Keeping Horses

Also from Blackwell Scientific Publications

Horse and Stable Management
Jeremy Houghton Brown and Vincent Powell-Smith
0–632–02141–1

Getting Horses Fit
Improve Your Horse's Performance
Second Edition
Sarah Pilliner
0–632–03476–9

Equine Injury and Therapy
Mary Bromiley
0–632–02277–9

How to Keep Your Horse Healthy
Colin Vogel
0–632–02056–3

Pasture Management for Horses and Ponies
Gillian McCarthy
0–632–02286–8

Horse Business Management
Jeremy Houghton Brown and Vincent Powell-Smith
0–632–02184–5

Practical Stud Management
John Rose an Sarah Pilliner
0–632–02031–8

The Equine Athlete
How to Develop Your Horse's Athletic Potential
Jo Hodges and Sarah Pilliner
0–632–02622–7

The Competition Horse
Breeding, Production and Management
Susan McBane with Gillian McCarthy
0–632–02327–9

Horse Nutrition and Feeding
Sarah Pilliner
0–632–03239–1

Keeping Horses

The Working Owner's Guide to Saving Time and Money

Second Edition

Susan McBane

OXFORD

BLACKWELL SCIENTIFIC PUBLICATIONS

LONDON EDINBURGH BOSTON

MELBOURNE PARIS BERLIN VIENNA

© Susan McBane 1986, 1993

Blackwell Scientific Publications
Editorial Offices:
Osney Mead, Oxford OX2 0EL
25 John Street, London WC1N 2BL
23 Ainslie Place, Edinburgh EH3 6AJ
238 Main Street, Cambridge,
  Massachusetts 02142, USA
54 University Street, Carlton
  Victoria 3053, Australia

Other Editorial Offices:
Librairie Arnette SA
2, rue Casimir-Delavigne
75006 Paris
France

Blackwell Wissenschafts-Verlag
Meinekestrasse 4
D-1000 Berlin 15
Germany

Blackwell MZV
Feldgasse 13
A-1238 Wien
Austria

First edition published in Great Britain by
Collins Professional and Technical Books
  1986
Reprinted 1987
Reprinted by BSP Professional Books
  1988, 1990, 1991
Second edition published by
Blackwell Scientific Publications 1993

Set by DP Photosetting, Aylesbury, Bucks
Printed and bound in Great Britain by
Hartnolls, Bodmin, Cornwall

DISTRIBUTORS

Marston Book Services Ltd
PO Box 87
Oxford OX2 0DT
(*Orders:* Tel: 0865 791155
      Fax: 0865 791927
      Telex: 837515)

USA
Blackwell Scientific Publications, Inc.
238 Main Street
Cambridge, MA 02142
((*Orders:* Tel: 800 759-6102
          617 876-7000)

Canada
Oxford University Press
70 Wynford Drive
Don Mills
Ontario M3C 1J9
(*Orders:* Tel: 416 441-2941)

Australia
Blackwell Scientific Publications
Pty Ltd
54 University Street
Carlton, Victoria 3053
(*Orders:* Tel: 03 347-5552)

British Library
Cataloguing in Publication Data
A Catalogue record for this book is
available from the British Library

√ISBN 0–632–03443–2

Library of Congress
Cataloging in Publication Data
McBane, Susan.
    Keeping horses : the working owner's
  guide to saving time and money /
  Susan McBane. — 2nd ed.
      p. cm.
    Includes index.
    ISBN 0–632–03443–2
    1. Horses. I. Title.
  SF285.3.M42   1993
  636.1′08′3—dc20   92–27932
                                      CIP

This book is dedicated to

ROY

a working horse owner who never seems
to have any time or money

Contents

Preface to the first edition

There is not one domesticated animal I can think of which takes up quite so much time and money in its care as does the horse. Even dogs, particularly house dogs who are part of the family and who boss their humans into spending all their spare time playing with them and taking them for walkies, do not involve us in so many time-consuming essential chores, and certainly do not cost so much to keep as do horses.

This book has been written mainly for working horse owners, that increasing band of people who have to work not only to keep themselves but to keep their horse or horses, too. Because they have to work to keep the horse, they do not have the time to do all the tasks necessary to a horse's care as they feel they should be done. Also, from a financial point of view, how many times have you heard the comment from a non-horsy friend or acquaintance: 'You must be doing well to be able to afford a horse!' and vainly tried to explain that it is precisely *because* you have a horse that you are, in fact, hard up most of the time?

Time and money – these are two commodities working owners are often short of yet which horses need a lot of. In my experience, many people become bogged down in other people's standards, other people's ideas of what is right and wrong in horse-management. Many of us in Britain are too conformist for our horses' good, too worried about doing things by 'The Book' and are consequently rushed off our feet most of the time as we try to fit in a job, a horse, domestic responsibilities, family and some kind of social life.

There are, however, many ways in which we can cut down on the work involved in caring for a horse (not to mention a house) and in which we can cut down on the expense involved, too.

It is hoped that the ideas and tips given in this book, accumulated over years of experience as a working owner, will provide both food for thought and practical help for other working owners everywhere.

Susan McBane

Preface to the second edition

It is only six years since this book was first published but the need for it seems to have increased even more. Britain, along with other countries, has been experiencing a recession for the past few years and economics in time and money have become more necessary than ever.

This new edition of *Keeping Horses* has been completely revised and updated in line with present prices and practices in the horse world. In particular, I hope the list of cash saving tips (Chapter 3) will provide further ideas in this essential area of horse management for owners to make the very best of their budgets and buying power, and that the flow charts on various disorders will help owners make an accurate decision as to whether or not a veterinary surgeon is needed or whether the matter can wait, so saving on the cost of a visit from the vet – a not insignificant expense these days. On the other hand, the charts should also make clearer those occasions when a visit is essential for the wellbeing of the horse.

From the comments I have received from readers of the first edition of this book as to its encouraging and down-to-earth tone and helpful content, I do hope this second edition will be even more useful and inspiring not only to working owners but anyone who simply does not have all day to attend to their horse or horses. It *is* possible to juggle a job, family, social life and horses without any of them suffering and this book will show you how. The section on prioritising jobs remains one of the most important in the book and is the real key to keeping a horse truly well cared for on limited time and money.

Acknowledgements

I should first like to thank Sue Triggs for executing the line drawings which have enhanced this book and have provided both explanation and decoration. She has depicted actual facilities known to the author but which she herself has not seen and has done an excellent job under less than ideal conditions. Lt Col. Anthony Crossley also readily provided ideas and information concerning his own system of management which have been incorporated in the book. The guidance, patience and lunches provided by my editor, Julian Grover, have also been much appreciated. Finally, I should like to thank the following organisations and commercial concerns for providing information and photographs:

Personalite Ltd, PO Box 45, Barnet, EN5 4NA. Tel: (081) 449 9117

KEW Industry Ltd, KEW House, Gilwilly Industrial Estate, Penrith, CA11 9BN. Tel: (0768) 65777

Equestrian Security Services, 17 St John's Road, Farnham, Surrey, GU9 8NU

Lavenham Rug Co. Ltd, Long Melford, CO10 9JL. Tel: (0787) 79535

Equitus Ltd, Burnt Ash House, Cirencester Road, Chalford, Stroud, GL6 8PE. Tel: (0453) 882272

Faulks & Jaques, 27 Innage Park, Holly Lane, Atherstone, CV9 2HA. Tel: (08277) 67003

ADAS Unit, Ministry of Agriculture, Fisheries & Food, National Agricultural Centre, Kenilworth, CV8 2LG. Tel: (0203) 57112

British Trust for Conservation Volunteers, 36 St. Mary's Street, Wallingford, OX10 0EU. Tel: (0491) 39766

Messrs Weatherbys, 42 Portman Square, London, W1H 0EN. Tel: (071) 486 4921

Mr G. Asker, Kings Barn Farm, Medmenham, Marlow, Bucks. Tel: (0491) 571400

Equequip Ltd, 7 Pepper Alley, Banbury, OX16 0TF. Tel: (0295) 3913

Ridry, Cobbacombe Farm, Huntsham, Tiverton, EX16 7QJ. Tel: (0398) 31711

Acorn Rugs, Gairsheild Farm, Steel, Hexham, NE47 0HS. Tel: (0434) 73562

Loddon Livestock Equipment Ltd, Loddon, Norwich, NR14 6JJ. Tel: (0508) 20744

Greenham Saddlery Co. Ltd, Ridge House, Greenham, Wellington, TA2 10JS. Tel: (0823) 672304

Your Horse magazine, Bretton Court, Bretton, Peterborough, PE3 8DZ. Tel: (0733) 264666

Caledonian Fencing Ltd, Phoenix Works, North Street, Lewes, Sussex. Tel: (0273) 477118

Susan McBane

1 Managing yourself and your horse

There is a very well-worn saying in the horse world and one which is very true: it says 'each horse is an individual and must be treated as such'. It is also true that there are certain set methods and procedures when looking after horses which are widely accepted and used and which are detailed in most good books on horse management. Between this individuality of any particular horse and the uniformity of method of a set system of management lies the secret of keeping a horse happy, healthy and well cared for.

A method which suits one animal perfectly may be anathema to another, and it is the owner's or attendant's ability to adapt existing systems of management to suit his or her particular horse, facilities and circumstances which determines how successful he or she will be as a horsemaster.

In the case of a horse owner who can spend only limited time looking after a horse because of work and other commitments, it is particularly important that the horse and the system adopted are compatible because the owner will not be there most of the time to cater to the horse's needs if he is not very happy about something. It is no use, for example, trying to make an active, athletic type of horse who is always full of energy (nervous or otherwise) exist under a system where he spends twenty-three out of his twenty-four hours stabled. It would also be somewhat unsatisfactory to keep out the type of animal who curls up at the first sign of wind or rain.

Let us, therefore, look at the various systems of horse management, the advantages and disadvantages of each and how we can relate them to horses' differing constitutions and temperaments.

Stabling

Keeping a horse entirely or almost entirely stabled is obviously the
most tying and time-consuming way of keeping him. It is not,
however, necessarily much more expensive than yarding a horse or
keeping him at grass as both those facilities may have to be rented;
yarded horses have to be fed as stabled horses all year round and
in winter grass-kept horses will probably need more food than
stabled ones to keep out the cold.

A stabled horse has to have everything done for him by his
human attendants and it may be very difficult for an owner with
limited time to give a stabled horse enough exercise (in particular)
to keep him healthy. Every day a healthy horse, even an unfit one,
needs a minimum of two hours' exercise to maintain his health.
This does not necessarily mean ridden or driven exercise, but
general moving about either at will or being led, lunged or long-
reined, as the case may be. He needs to be groomed to prevent
excessive build-up of dandruff and grease in his coat as he is not
exposed to rain, his stable has to be mucked out – not only for
physical reasons because hygiene has to be maintained, but also for
mental reasons as horses in general dislike being near their own
droppings, he has to be fed by us regularly and frequently, and
also maybe have clothing attended to. So time and convenience are
at a premium in caring for stabled horses.

The advantages of keeping a horse stabled are that it is relatively
easy to keep him clean as he will not be able to coat himself in
mud, the horse is always handy when needed, he can be kept fitter
than a grass-kept horse (although a yarded horse can be just as fit)
and we can control his diet minutely, if required. This latter point
is important in horses whose work is physically demanding and
who cannot perform at their optimum level if eating too much
grass.

Keeping a Horse at Grass

Seen by many as the most natural system of horse keeping, the
outdoor life does, however, have many disadvantages for both
horse and owner. Some 'artificial' breeds of horse such as the
Thoroughbred, and others which originate from hot climates (such

as Arabs and other oriental breeds), often do not thrive when out in cold, wet, windy weather. Such thin-skinned animals are prone not only to exposure in winter but to unbearable attacks from insects in summer. Some animals suffer badly from mud fever and rain rash in appropriate conditions and, despite shelter sheds and New Zealand rugs, simply cannot stand being out in a cold field.

'Outdoor' horses can, of course, exercise themselves at will, although they tend not to do so when miserable. They can eat grass, drink when they please (a source permitting), enjoy the company of their own kind and develop natural social relationships in most cases – something denied stabled animals and those (such as stallions) kept away from other horses.

From their attendants' point of view, such horses are not quite as tying as stabled horses, although they should be seen twice daily to check on their general well-being, for feeding if necessary and so that action can be taken in case of accidents, kicks and the like. A certain amount of grooming should be done – at least discharges from eyes and nostrils should be assessed and sponged away, feet should be picked out and shoes, if worn, checked – and New Zealand rugs, when worn, should be frequently re-adjusted and changed.

Provided grass-kept horses are on grazing of fairly low nutritional content (although clean and well cared for), they can be kept quite fit – as proved by many endurance horses, despite the fact that it is held by most authorities to be impossible to keep them as fit as stabled horses. Except in dry weather they cannot, certainly, be kept as clean as their stabled colleagues, which is unlikely to worry them but may worry their owners. In winter, as mentioned, they may well eat more food than stabled horses, and it is certainly not so convenient to care for them outdoors in bad weather unless they can be tied up in their shelter or somewhere under cover.

The Combined System

Many authorities believe this to be the best system of keeping any horse. It is simply a combination of stabling and turning out a horse who spends some of his time stabled and some out. The system is very flexible, the number of hours in and out varying according to daily circumstances.

The advantages and disadvantages of the system are simply

those of the other two systems; in practice, the combined system works very well indeed because the horse can have the freedom of an outdoor life but with the warmth and shelter of his stable, when needed. He can be kept as fit as any stabled horse, but because he can also be turned out he is not as tying to his owner as a stabled animal. Feed and bedding can be saved according to time of year and length of time out although grazing may have to be rented.

The combined system is ideal for avoiding those extremes of both the other systems which bring their own problems – exposure and cold in winter in susceptible individuals and excess heat and insect attacks in summer with the outdoor system, and the boredom, frustration and inner tension, resulting in various vices and other physical and mental problems, which can occur when horses are kept fully stabled even when they are given what we consider to be adequate exercise.

Horses rarely appreciate extremes of either of the first two systems, in my experience, and because of its obvious practical advantages, I am a great fan of the combined system.

Yarding

Another system increasingly used in Great Britain and Ireland and common in some other countries is yarding; it is used not only for breeding stock and resting horses but also for horses in work. Horses are kept in dirt enclosures, partly or fully roofed, so have the freedom to exercise themselves as much as space will allow but with the advantage of significant shelter. Sometimes the enclosure is a yard in front of a large, open-fronted shed which is bedded down and the horse or horses can come and go as they wish. In other cases, a single stable may have a smaller yard leading from it which simply permits the horse to walk about and have a measure of freedom.

Facilities used vary considerably and the system has much to recommend it because it gives horses some freedom without entailing the disadvantages of their being out at grass. The dirt yards normally used will not support grass in any quantity, so horses are fed as stabled horses.

'Corralling' is a system used in the U.S.A. and some other countries, and is a system closely allied to yarding except that the horses do not have shelter. They are kept in a high-fenced pen and fed by their attendants as stabled horses but do have the freedom to exercise themselves. The corral is also often used for schooling purposes.

Which System for You and Your Horse?

The choice of a suitable system depends on several things. Most important of these is your horse's constitution and temperament. As briefly mentioned earlier, neither of you will be happy if you choose the wrong method. If you have a highly-strung horse always wanting to be on the go but you have only the time to give him an hour or two's work each day, it will not be surprising if he develops one or more stable vices or other mental or physical problems should you decide to keep him more or less fully stabled. On the other hand, a thin-skinned, hot-blooded type of animal will be thoroughly miserable and will suffer considerably, mentally and physically, if he is wintered out without proper facilities (shelter, clothing and ample feeding), and maybe even with them.

It would be helpful if we could say what breeds and types do best under what systems, but there is so much individual variance that the only reliable advice which can be given is 'know your own horse'. There *are* many Thoroughbred and Arab type horses who winter out happily given good facilities; likewise, just because a cob is normally regarded as a placid type of animal, not particularly sensitive to the elements and not given to wanting to be on the go all the time, it does not mean that all cobs can live out with equanimity all year round or, conversely, stay happily stabled most of the time on limited exercise.

It is essential to really get to know your horse as an individual, to understand his mental and physical needs and tendencies, so that you can try to accommodate him in the most suitable way. Unhappy horses do not thrive and can cost more to keep than contented ones. Those who develop vices such as crib-biting, wind-sucking and eating foreign matter (e.g. wood and droppings) often develop digestive troubles which mean food is not being utilised as well as it could be. This is a waste of money, and such vices can actually result in colic, which means further expense on veterinary bills. Those who develop other vices such as weaving and box-walking may, again, be poor doers, not least because they are using physical energy all the time.

On the other hand, horses exposed to cold, wet conditions and who are not able to stand up to them expend tremendous energy just trying to keep warm – again, a waste of money which stabling and a good rug would obviate.

There is no other answer to the question of choosing the right system than to be guided mainly by the horse's needs. As a working owner, particularly one without his or her own facilities who has to keep a horse on someone else's premises, either at livery or in rented accommodation, you may not have too much choice over where you keep your horse. But I feel it is better to have peace of mind for both of you and to keep your horse, say, a little further from your home than you would normally wish and know he is being accommodated according to his requirements, than to have him handy but forced to put up with conditions which make him unhappy and worry you.

Your own working hours, domestic commitments and the time you spend commuting to and from work will also have a bearing on just how much time you can spend on your horse and will, therefore, govern to some extent the management system you adopt. I would venture to suggest, however, that if your time availability, or lack of it, is such that you cannot spare the four hours or so a day it takes to exercise, groom, muck out, feed and otherwise look after a stabled horse, then do not consider this system of management – or, in fact, the type of horse who cannot stand to be out in winter for long hours while you are at work. If he is miserable he will not exercise himself and so help to keep himself warm, but will mope by the gate, getting colder and colder and more and more unhappy, until you or someone else appears to bring him in.

Only you can really assess the situation, depending on your horse and your other circumstances.

Where to Keep Your Horse

Most horse and pony owners in the U.K. have to keep their animals on someone else's property. They do so usually because they do not have the facilities needed (land, stabling, fodder storage, etc.) at home, but some do so because they are unable or unwilling to give the time and daily commitment needed when doing a horse oneself; such owners, therefore, keep their horses at full or part livery, normally at a riding school or livery stable.

There is a method which comes between these two systems and that is doing your horse yourself but not at home, i.e. in rented accommodation. Let us look at these three sources of accommodation.

At Home

For many owners, this is the best way to keep a horse. It is much more convenient, certainly, than having to travel to your horse, you can normally be sure that no one is 'tampering' with him while you are not present and because you, and possibly your family, look after him yourselves you can be certain that he is cared for according to your requirements.

However, if you are keeping your horse at home and doing him entirely yourself, with no family help, it is extremely tying unless you can get occasional, possibly paid, help when you are ill or away.

If you do not have suitable facilities at home they will have to be created, and while many owners rent grazing near their homes they go to all sorts of ingenious lengths to provide stabling on their own property. Provided your horse is not a nuisance to neighbours (for instance, breaking into their gardens, eating their flowers over the fence, creating unreasonable noise or smells) there may, in fact, be little they can do about it because you are allowed under the Town and Country Planning Act 1971 and its subsequent General Development Order Statutory Instrument 1977/289 to build a stable adjoining your house and have it treated as an enlargement of the property provided it does not exceed one-tenth of the cubic area of the original dwelling house, or fifty cubic metres, subject to a maximum of 115 cubic metres.

You will have to get sight of your deeds, if you do not hold them yourself, to check that the property has not already been enlarged from its original size to the maximum permitted (for instance, if an extension has been built). Your stable cannot be higher than the highest part of the original dwelling and cannot protrude beyond the front line of the building where it fronts on to a highway.

It is probably best to consult your solicitor first on this matter rather than your local planning department who might be, as some have been, not merely unhelpful but actually obstructive and misleading. When you come to erect the stable, you will need plans and expert advice as to the actual siting of it; drainage and other health and safety matters need on-the-spot attention and local by-laws on such matters change from district to district. Basically, though, you will have to pay attention to such things as drainage and smells (already mentioned), fire risk where hay and straw or other inflammable materials are on site, whether heavy lorries are going to be visiting your premises frequently to deliver feed and bedding (and the access for them) and whether the horse or horses can break out and cause a nuisance to others or accidents on the road.

Even taking into account the cost of providing 'at home' facilities, your day-to-day costs will be less than keeping the horse anywhere else because you will have no rent or livery charges to pay – and, of course, the stable or stables and ancillary buildings will add to the value of your property if they are well and tastefully constructed (although possibly adding to your Council Tax bill, too!).

If you live in a residential area, you will have to give serious thought to the siting of the muck heap. In fact, if you can put the actual droppings straight into sacks which you then staple or tape up ready for sale (or giving away, if you must), you will obviate many of the problems of flies and smells which go with muck heaps. The used bedding minus droppings could be used to floor an exercise area, if you have room. Alternatively, you could arrange with a local nursery to take the muck away very frequently. In this case, the heap will have to be sited not only as far from houses as possible but where the nursery's lorry can get to it.

From the horse's point of view, the main disadvantages of living at your home may be lack of turn-out facilities and lack of company. You may be able to remedy the first by means of plenty of exercise and by providing an area just big enough for him to have a good roll and kick up his heels when he wants – almost anything is better than being stabled all the time. Lack of company may not be so easy to cope with and he may form a friendship with your family dog or some other animal.

It is better to give him other equine company if at all possible, perhaps by letting off a stable to a friend. Many horses, however, live quite happily if they are turned out on nearby grazing with other horses, just coming home to be stabled at night or whenever needed.

Fig. 1 'Almost anything is better than being stabled all the time.' This picture shows two former bull boxes with their pens in front which are being successfully used for horses. The doors are left open nearly all the time; the horses wear appropriate clothing when weather conditions demand, and spend most of their time outdoors. Access to the boxes is through side doors, there being no way in and out of the pens. There are windows in the back walls and the side top-doors and windows are also left open for ventilation, according to conditions. The central wall between the pens has been retained in case crowding problems occur should both horses try to get into one loose box. Although the pens are only slightly bigger than the boxes, they provide the horses with that extra room and remove the sense of imprisonment which so many stabled horses experience. There is everything to be said for providing such a facility in suitable locations in front of existing boxes, perhaps with an access gate in the front wall of the pen where there is only one door to the box. Ordinary fencing could, of course, be used instead of brick and iron bars.

At Livery

Time is money, and it is sometimes necessary to spend one in order to save the other. With livery arrangements, you are spending money to save time because, in theory at least, if you are paying full-livery charges for your horse there should never be any actual *need* for you to go and see him at all – you do so simply because you want to see him and be with him or to ride or drive him.

Different yards have different ideas of what constitutes full livery, but it *should* include stabling, bedding, grooming, feeding and watering and adequate exercise according to the horse's state of health and fitness. I feel that, where the facility exists, grazing should be included in the cost because, although it does cost money to maintain grazing, most yards save on feed when horses are out, even if only one feed/hay ration a day. However, many yards charge extra for grazing and many do not give enough exercise, seeming to regard one hour a day, and nothing else, as adequate. In practice, many yards will exercise your horse on four days a week, assuming you will be riding two days (weekends, normally) and the horse will be having one day off. So all the exercise they give is four hours a week, which is not very much by anyone's standards. If the horse can be turned out for at least half a day in addition, this might suffice – otherwise it will be quite inadequate to maintain a healthy horse in reasonable mental and physical health.

If you want more exercise (assuming it is available in terms of manpower and time), you will have to pay for it. If the yard has a mechanical horse-walker, this will at least stretch the horse's legs and should cost a bit less than 'personal' exercise. Although the machine uses electricity, it can exercise upwards of four horses at once, depending on design, and requires only one person to supervise. As with lunging, half an hour on a horse walker is enough for any horse.

You will have to pay extra for shoeing, schooling, veterinary expenses, tack and other equipment (although not normally such equipment as mucking-out tools) and also, where appropriate, travelling costs, plus insurance. Tack cleaning should also be included. Clipping is usually extra. You may have to pay extra for using a cross-country course, show jumps or for using an indoor school or other exercise facilities for a given number of hours. Ask if there are any extra charges in addition to those mentioned and on top of your livery fee. Check the security of the tackroom and yard in general as thefts of horses and equipment are on the increase. Also look at the flooring and safety of boarding or fencing of indoor or outdoor exercise areas, checking for stones, uneven going, holes and so on and excessive dust. It is also as well to ask if there is a latest time you are allowed in the yard, if only to visit your horse.

At the time of writing, full livery charges vary, according to the area of the country, from roughly £40 to £75 per week.

Half livery is cheaper, obviously, because you get fewer services. Most half-livery clients simply choose stabling, grazing, bedding, feeding and watering and basic grooming but not, normally, exercising or tack cleaning.

Where you keep your horse at livery at a riding centre, you will be charged less if you allow your horse to be used 'in the school', i.e. for students and selected clients to ride or drive. Unfortunately, it often works out that they need your horse when you want him; also, it is never good for a horse to have too many people working him, especially novices, so such arrangements should be gone into with care.

Choosing a livery yard for your horse can be quite difficult. Good places are extremely rare in some areas and many owners are in the unfortunate position of having to take more or less what they can get. As mentioned earlier, it is in practice worth a small fortune in peace of mind to keep your horse further away from home at a good place rather than at a poorer one closer by.

To assess a yard, simply judge the condition of the horses – not only their physical condition but their mental attitude, too. Are they correctly fed or thin or over-fat? Are they reasonably clean even when out of work or have they obviously not had a brush or sponge near them for days? Are they calm and interested in their surroundings, with contented, alert expressions, or are they miserable-looking, not bothering to look out of their boxes (indeed, are they *able* to look out of their boxes?), with too many of them showing obviously suspect tempers?

As for their general management, are rugs clean and well fitting, beds thick and clean whatever bedding material is used and boxes light and airy and plenty big enough for each animal (depending on his size) to lie fully flat out – which horses need to do to sleep – and lie down, get up and turn round in comfort? These are the important points to watch for. Also look out for left feed, particularly hay. Make a point of examining the hay to see, and smell, its quality. Horses only leave good hay when they have had quite enough. If the hay left is poor and/or sour, horses will leave it even though they are still hungry, and could then resort to eating foreign substances like wood, droppings and bedding. Check, too, that water containers, and the water in them, are clean.

Things like a slightly untidy yard or tack room, paintwork in need of attention and a muck heap which is less than immaculate do not matter much. Hopefully, this shows that more attention is paid to the horses themselves than to matters which do not *directly* affect the horses.

Human relationships are important, too. You could find life somewhat difficult if you keep your horse at a place run by people you cannot talk to or do not much like. Approachable, understanding, trustworthy, knowledgeable people are well worth seeking out. Remember, a bad atmosphere in a yard due to poor personal relationships may reflect on the horses, who can certainly sense it; their sense of security (essential to their happiness) could well be affected to the detriment of their well-being.

'Do-it-yourself livery' is simply a term for keeping your horse in rented accommodation and caring for him entirely yourself. You simply pay for stabling and (possibly separately) grazing, and buy all your own feed, bedding, equipment and do your own work. Such arrangements are the next cheapest alternative to keeping your horse at home but take up more time than having the horse outside your own back door because of the travelling time (and possibly expense if you can't walk or go on a bike) involved in visiting the horse at least twice a day. However, such arrangements seem to be becoming more and more common as keep and livery charges rise faster than salaries, and chapter 4 deals with communal livery and renting schemes in which friends and families help each other out as regards the work involved.

When choosing accommodation for such an arrangement, the facilities (stabling, grazing and individual storage areas for each client, not to mention a decent, secure tack room) are really what matter, as the condition of the individual horses and ponies present is controlled by their owners. However, if you visit a place where the animals largely seem not to be too well cared for, perhaps you should look elsewhere. Not only are these the type of owners on whom you might well be relying for help more or less frequently,

Fig. 2 There are various ways to stable horses and ponies without using strictly conventional stable complexes. This drawing shows a mare and foal in what used to be housing for young cattle. It has undergone no conversion at all. The broken windows were replaced by translucent rigid polythene. The wooden hayracks separating the 'boxes' give large communal supplies of hay which can be reached by animals on both sides. The animals can see each other through the bars, increasing their sense of company. Under the racks run the original mangers which are now used for the horses; they catch bits of hay which fall down and which might otherwise be wasted. (The haynets shown can provide a supplementary supply although they are not actually recommended for foals who might, in their antics, catch a hoof in the mesh.) This sort of stabling is ideal for housing in one box several temperamentally compatible ponies. The entrances are in an aisle to the right, out of the picture, and attendants have the advantage of working under cover in this little unit. This is an excellent example of providing good housing without expense.

but the state of their animals might well get on your nerves to the extent that your own contentment and satisfaction with your lot are adversely affected – it certainly does happen.

It may be possible to get your horse cared for and accommodated free or simply for the cost of his feed and bedding if he acts as companion to another horse. Many owners who work alone would welcome some part-time help too, and you could come to a mutual agreement over stable work for the benefit of you and your horses.

You may be lucky enough to find premises rent free if you undertake to put and keep them in good repair, although a written agreement would be a good idea. If you are of the entrepreneurial type, you could rent a yard and then charge others rent, not only covering your costs but making a profit as well, particularly if you can act as manager.

Finally, when choosing a yard, location should be considered. If you want to spend your time hacking rather than riding in a manège, for instance, it is no use keeping your horse at a yard in the middle of a traffic blackspot or surrounded by dangerous roads. Or if you wish to improve your and your horse's prowess across country, it could be inconvenient if there is no facility for cross-country riding either on the premises or nearby.

Income and Expenditure

It is necessary to weigh all the factors and try to end up with your horse in a yard (or at your home) where he will be well cared for by you, by staff or by other owners, friends or family members, which has the facilities you need for your particular equestrian discipline and which is neither too inconvenient to get too nor too expensive for your income. It is usually worth paying a little extra for what you want and being happy, rather than scrimping and saving small amounts and ending up with an unsatisfactory arrangement.

2 A year in your life: an overview

The equestrian sporting year never stops but simply turns full circle; only the different equestrian disciplines have their seasons, and some are only divided into an indoor season (in winter) and an outdoor season (in summer), notably show jumping and, to a lesser extent, novice-level showing. For the owner of the 'all-purpose' horse, there are more than enough equestrian activities to take part in to keep horse and owner occupied all year round.

In spring some hunting will still be going on, the show season has started with its various disciplines such as showing classes (in-hand, ridden and driven) and ancillary events such as combined training, gymkhanas, and the sports of eventing, endurance riding and combined driving will have their spring seasons. Point-to-pointing, having started in February, will still be going on, although this is hardly a suitable outlet for most 'ordinary' horses and their owners.

Summer sees polo joining the scene, including Pony Club polo. In autumn, cub-hunting will start and there is the autumn season for eventing, driving trials and endurance riding. Winter sees hunting proper in full swing or can be taken up with getting fit for spring competitions of various kinds. There are Riding Club shows and other events, team chasing, private driving, hunter trials, dressage and maybe instructional courses and clinics. For those who just like to ride for the sake of it, without competing or hunting, there is, of course, hacking all year round and hacking can be as placid or strenuous as you want it to be, depending, admittedly, on local facilities.

Whatever work your horse is to do, he has to be made fit and to be cared for appropriately for the task in hand. This book is not a manual on the specific topic of caring for a horse, but on how to save time and money in doing so. Readers are assumed to have a reasonable standard of knowledge, therefore, but perhaps a few words on the difficulties and advantages presented by each season of the year, and how they affect our preparation for various disciplines, will not go amiss.

It is worth noting, first, that it takes less time and effort to *keep* a horse fit than to actually get him fit. The type of horse mainly under consideration in this book, the all-round, family-type or Riding Club horse, will probably be in work most of the year and will, therefore, spend most of his year, say, three-quarters fit (if we take fully fit as racing or three-day-eventing fit). This is a considerable advantage because this type of fitness is quite adequate for what you will want him to do and can be maintained by the horse's normal work plus a bit extra. It is also better for his general health to be always partially fit like this than to be allowed to get fat and soft in summer or thin and run down in winter.

To restore a horse to reasonable fitness from either of those two conditions needs a lot of time, slow work, patience and skill in feeding and judgement of changing physical condition. Without those qualities, it is easy to over-stress an unfit horse and end up with legs which won't withstand the season because they weren't given enough slow roadwork at the beginning of a fitness programme, or slight heart strain because fast work, even short pipe-openers, was begun too soon or carried on too long.

The horse who is always fairly fit is less susceptible to stresses and strains during the normal course of his work, healthier (provided his general care is correct and appropriate) and less prone to work-related accidents and even to accidents in the field. Because his body is 'tuned up', he can use it better to get out of scrapes such as uneven ground or a tree which suddenly looms up and needs dodging or a companion who decides to have a mad half hour and chivvy everybody else in the paddock.

There is, of course, no substitute for acquiring as much knowledge as possible and being able to manage one's horse or horses under all conditions and in all states of well-being – but generally speaking a horse who is fairly fit and in work most of the year is less of a liability to his owner than one whose condition varies significantly with the seasons.

Seasons of the Year

For most working owners and their horses, winter is the most difficult time of year. The worst part of a British winter, apart from the dark which makes exercising difficult, is the wet. Nine times out of ten when you go out to exercise, you will get soaked and so will your horse. The wet also often brings with it mud fever and rain scald (dealt with in chapter 7) and often makes turn-out facilities, particularly small, overcrowded or badly drained ones, unusable due to poaching or simply standing water.

Wet combined with cold and wind can have a very serious chilling effect on horses with inadequate shelter, even when they are well fed. Such conditions are just as miserable for the human side of the partnership, although both can obtain a good deal of protection and comfort from well-fitting waterproof clothing.

You will certainly have your work cut out to look after a clipped, corn-fed horse adequately in winter if you are also working and/or have other time-consuming commitments such as looking after a house and family. If you have a nine-to-five job, it may only just be getting light when you have to leave the horse and set off for work, and it will certainly be dark again when you return. Somehow, exercising on light summer evenings doesn't seem like a chore at all, whereas the same task during identical hours on a dark winter night is exactly that. A stabled, corn-fed horse involves just as much work, winter or summer, but in winter that work does seem more onerous!

There are, of course, dangers inherent in taking out a horse on public roads after dark although, as discussed in chapter 7, much can be done to lessen them. However, many owners feel that their winter burden is lightened if their horse can be turned out during the time they are at work, even if only for a few hours a day.

There may be times in winter when freezing conditions make road exercise, or any other work-type exercise, ridden or driven, almost impossible, so this can create more work in the way of laying down manure tracks for riding or lunging on, and then clearing them away again when the thaw comes.

If the weather freezes significantly (rather than just hovering around freezing point) this can, in fact, make turn-out areas more acceptable. Horses used to being turned out anyway are normally quite safe if turned on to frozen fields as, being accustomed to being out, they will not go charging about like lunatics. They quickly sense the state of the ground and move accordingly.

Freezing weather creates sometimes major difficulties in watering horses, even stabled ones. Underground pipes need to be at least 30 cm (1 ft) deep if they are to escape all but the worst frost, and those above ground have to be lagged. Horses in fields must have their water containers cleared of ice at least twice daily, and some horses refuse to drink out of a container which has broken ice floating on the top, anyway. If such horses have their water supplied by hosepipe, you have to be sure to bring the hosepipe

Fig. 3 This shows a top quality field shelter such as is sold by many stabling manufacturers. It is sited on the highest (and therefore driest) part of the field with its back to the prevailing wind. A part-wall at the front might provide all-round shelter for when the wind changes direction but would also provide a corner into which one animal might hem another. The shelter is kept on deep litter bedding and the long hayrack running along the back is kept stocked up with hay except when the grazing is plentiful in late spring, summer and early autumn. This shelter has guttering and a downpipe to take the rainwater which would otherwise drip down the front and onto the horses if, like many, they had the habit of standing half in and half out of the shelter. There is no drain to take the water, but it creates no problems and drains away naturally. The shelter is built on a layer of bricks to help protect the lower timbers from ground damp. Much simpler shelters can be built using these principles – a single pitch roof sloping down from front to back would be cheaper and would do away with the need for the drainpipe and guttering. Second-hand timber could be used and haynets provided instead of a rack. The same aims re positioning, however, should be followed. Entrances should always be high, wide and welcoming so the horses are not deterred from entering the shelter.

indoors each night – if water freezes inside it you will be left with no means of getting water to outdoor horses (except carrying buckets).

Come to think of it, I can find no actual advantages to winter except that there aren't any insects to bother the horses.

Spring, on the other hand, definitely does have advantages. Longer daylight hours make exercising safer and more pleasant, although it can still be very cold in spring. The main disadvantage, once the grass starts coming through, is that if the grass is at all rich a surfeit can cause severe digestive and circulatory problems – colic and laminitis are both very painful and incapacitating and can, in fact, lead to the death of the horse; a horse can certainly die of a colic and severe cases of laminitis often result in a decision to put the animal down.

However, if the grass is of poor to medium quality and the horse is not totally unused to grass beforehand, long spring days out in the field while you are at work can be very pleasant for the horse and, as turning out usually is, labour saving for you from the point of view of exercising.

Care should be taken during early spring to watch for sudden deterioration in the weather and to equip the horse with his New Zealand rug, if necessary, particularly if he has been stabled and rugged up all winter. Otherwise, he will surely feel the cold and could lose condition.

Summer can, in two particular respects, be as miserable for the horse as winter. First, there are the problems caused by flies – I am sure that most owners do not realise (and some simply ignore) the agonies horses can go through when they are exposed to insects. It is worse during the daylight hours but there are night-flying insects, too, which bother horses.

Although nature does equip horses with various anti-fly devices, such as manes and tails and an extensive flat muscle under the skin of the back, sides and flanks with which he can twitch flies off those areas, to keep himself permanently free of their attentions he must keep up a ceaseless performance of head shaking, leg stamping, muscle twitching and tail swishing which is both mentally and physically wearying. In bad cases, flies drive horses to stampede around their paddocks, again exhausting and damaging in the case of an unfit animal. As horses do not see well when galloping fast this is dangerous, as they can collide with fencing, buildings, trees and other obstructions they would normally avoid, not least because their attention is more on the flies than on where they are going. Hard ground in summer also jars legs and breaks feet.

Sweet itch is a very distressing condition suffered in summer by horses allergic to the saliva of the *culicoides* midge which is active around sunrise and sunset. As treatment of established sweet itch is difficult and, apparently, hit-and-miss, the best method of dealing with it is prevention (dealt with, again, in chapter 7). This applies to all fly problems including bot flies and the now rare warble fly.

The second main problem in what we humans call a good summer is sun and heat which can distress horses considerably. Cool, shady areas provide a haven for them, particularly if they are out for many hours in daylight.

The advantages of summer include the temperature, which many humans, particularly the sun-seekers, love (no frozen fingers, cold rain or snow and ice to cope with). There is also no need to thatch the horse if he is wet unless the weather is really unseasonal, no time-consuming rugging-up or off-rugging, no being cluttered up with bulky clothing ourselves and, of course, there are long evenings and light mornings which, together with the temperature, make horse management and the chores that go with the enjoyment much easier and pleasanter.

Autumn brings a return to kinder conditions for horses. There are no extremes of heat or sun, flies gradually disappear and the ground softens, although in a very wet autumn, of course, it becomes muddy. The grass gives an autumn 'flush' of growth, too, but it is of low protein content, so if your horse is relying on grass for food at this time of year a protein supplement of some kind (depending on the advice of a specialist such as a veterinary surgeon or nutritionist) could be needed.

Nights start to draw in now, however, rugs could be needed and at this time of year fog often creates problems. Although it might be permissible to exercise a horse in dusk or dark conditions if suitably equipped with reflective clothing and a stirrup light (as discussed in chapter 7), fog is a definite no-no as far as I am concerned for taking horses on to the road, even if they are lit up like Christmas trees, so other means of exercising must be devised.

Holidays for Horse and Owner

Many horse owners fit their holidays around their equestrian activities but others like a complete break away from all routine aspects of their normal lives. Those in the latter category obviously have to make arrangements for the care of their horses while they are away.

Holidays for horses usually mean a period at grass so, from the horse's point of view, the best times of year to take a break are spring and/or autumn. Although the type of horse mostly being considered in this book may never be so tuned up that he becomes in dire need of a long rest, most horses do like to have a period at grass with no work provided it does not become too long and boring. A fortnight's break in spring and autumn to tie in with his owner's annual holiday entitlement seems ideal.

If you keep your horse at home and there is not going to be a suitably reliable, expert member of the family left at home to care for him, it would be more satisfactory for him to be sent for the period in question to a reputable livery centre or riding school, probably one approved by the British Horse Society and/or Association of British Riding Schools. In fact, if a rest is not called for and money is not too tight, this would be a good opportunity for the horse to receive a period of professional schooling.

If you keep your horse in a do-it-yourself livery yard, can you be absolutely certain that during your absence the other owners there will look after your horse in the manner to which he is accustomed, probably in exchange for your helping look after theirs in similar circumstances? If not, and you don't want the horse to go away to livery, your only alternative might be to employ a freelance groom to see to him morning and night while you are away.

Whatever arrangements you make, ensure that whoever is doing the honours while you are away has a telephone number where you can be reached in an emergency. If you are touring, you should ring up regularly and should, in any case, leave them the telephone number of your vet with authorisation to ring him or her, or any other vet of their choice in case yours is unavailable, should the need arise. The same goes for farriery problems – a neglected spread or loose shoe can soon cause a nasty accident.

Also leave detailed feeding information and, if the horse is going away, a supply of his own food, particularly hay or hay-age, so as not to cause digestive upsets which can come with a sudden change of feed.

Preparing for Different Disciplines

The basic preparation and conditioning for any equestrian activity is pretty much the same. If your horse is in work for most of the year, short breaks such as described above will not appreciably diminish his fitness, and you can subsequently carry on where you

Fig. 4 This picture shows how one end of a covered hay barn has been adapted as a covered yard with direct access to a paddock. The horses cannot reach the bales but have their own supply of hay, when called for, provided in racks around the perimeter. This facility provides for the horses' physical and mental needs and their owner finds them easily catered for. They both compete actively at Riding Club level and are trace clipped in winter and remain as fit as when they were mainly stabled in their previous accommodation, yet are far less trying for their owner.

left off after perhaps just a few days' gentle work to help his mind and body get the message that it's back to normal now.

It is a good idea to sit down with a year planner and plan out your year ahead. First put in the major events the horse is expected to attend and the times of his and your holidays. Also put in the times of yearly medical checks, vaccinations, teeth checks, blood tests or whatever are called for. Plan these well before any events as, especially in the case of vaccinations, many horses take a little while to get over them and feel below par for some days afterwards. Teeth rasping, too, can give a horse a sore mouth which may cause eating problems (so soft food should be given and hay-age or thoroughly steamed hay). Should the medical reveal a problem which needs attention, there will, hopefully, be time to deal with it before The Day if adequate time is allowed when planning your yearly programme.

With this basic information in front of you, you will have a clear picture of the horse's changing work pattern and, thus, of your own throughout the year. It does not always follow that when he is working hardest you will be too, for more rest days can be allowed so you will not necessarily be spending more time exercising. However, getting everything down on paper in an organised plan lets you see your year more easily, and what is involved, enabling your daily and weekly workloads to be worked out.

Consider, also, your precise method of management for each season in relation to the activities you are going to undertake. If you are going to spend the winter with the horse out during the day Monday to Friday and just hack about at weekends, does the horse really need clipping, even with a trace or Irish clip? An unclipped horse, with or without a New Zealand rug, can withstand long days out in the field while you are at work much better than a clipped one, and will need less food and clothing to keep him warm. However, if you are going to hunt on Saturdays and probably work the horse on a couple of days in the week to maintain fitness, too, some kind of clip will be needed to prevent excessive sweating and to facilitate care and cleaning afterwards.

In summer, when this category of horse normally works hardest, he will need to be quite fit for perhaps strenuous weekends and evening hacks or instructional classes. You have the daylight in your favour now, but if you should be in the unusual (for the average horse owner) position of having rich, plentiful grazing available, facilities will have to be secured and arrangements made to have the horse brought in for much of the time (say, during the day away from the flies) to reduce his grass intake. Otherwise, he will become too fat to do your work comfortably and safely, not to mention being at risk from the other problems of rich grazing.

By giving careful thought to your horse's individual constitution and temperament (both of which have an important bearing on his management) and to your own working times on a daily and yearly basis, plus the various equestrian activities you wish to take part in, you will be able to plan your year to best advantage, see quickly what is going to be involved during each season and so organise yourself accordingly.

The key to fitness and to maintaining soundness, particularly leg soundness, in any horse is adequate preparation in the 'slow' stages of a fitness programme – and this applies whether you are using interval training or more traditional methods of conditioning a horse. A fitness programme of whatever type, for whatever discipline, cannot be rushed. If it is skirr̃ed it is simply not performed. The type of programme you use will depend on your horse's mental and physical constitution and the type of work he is going to do.

For example, animals aimed at pursuits where hard, muscled-up fitness is not required can safely be given a slightly shorter walking period at the beginning of a fitness programme – a fortnight instead of a month should be adequate for children's ponies and horses not doing much hard or fast work or a lot of jumping. Riding Club work, showing, dressage, private driving and hacking come into this category. For animals expected to do strenuous work such as eventing, polo, racing of any kind, driving trials and endurance work, a month of walking work, culminating in about three hours a day with the horse walking properly up to his bridle most of the time, but with odd periods of relaxation, should be allowed and fitted into the year planner.

When trotting is introduced on roads, it should be no more than a working trot. Some experts claim that no horse should trot on the road while others maintain that it helps harden legs and feet. My experience is that it is beneficial, and certainly not harmful, *provided* the trot *is* a steady one. If you have the kind of horse who will not walk on happily once he starts to get fit but wants to keep trotting before you feel he is ready, try to find softer ground for the trotting such as verges, a field, manège or the beach, whatever is appropriate to your circumstances. Again, provided the trotting is steady and limited in the early stages, it is better to let the horse trot on a bit and be happy than to keep nagging at him to slow down and perhaps spoil his urge to give you free, forward movement!

The further conditioning of your horse again depends on his job, and the horse who will take up most time is the endurance horse as long rides must become part of his routine to harden and accustom him to bearing tack and weight for long periods. (He must also be trained to lead easily in hand for those spells when you travel off his back to rest it and to loosen up your own limbs.)

Racehorses of different categories will have short canters with the length, speed and frequency of work-outs increasing until the horse is ready to race. His first race should bring him on in fitness, not take anything out of him. If it does, he was not ready for it. Event horses need to start specific dressage schooling and athletic jumping as well as long canters to build up stamina. Like endurance horses, they must become accustomed to covering distances relevant to their competitive goals.

Horses in these categories may begin interval training proper at this stage, although few racehorses are conditioned by this method. The system does not lend itself to excitable horses, with its constant stopping and starting, but can benefit and sharpen up the stuffier sorts.

Show jumpers, show horses and dressage horses need correct flat work to build up their muscles, develop obedience and develop their agility and 'gymnastic' prowess, the jumpers also needing athletic jumping practice, like the eventers. It is often a good idea to combine hacks with dressage training to avoid the boredom of being 'drilled'. It is surprising how many professional yards do not have a manège or 'formal' schooling area as such but use their own paddocks, local bridleways and lanes, taking advantage of every handy facility such as the odd fallen tree, uneven ground to develop balance, making sure the horse goes correctly round bends, bending in and out of trees and the like.

Provided the grass is not rich, certainly the slow stage of a fitness programme can be carried out from the field. The old-fashioned practice of bringing horses up suddenly (without reducing grass and gradually introducing hard feed while the horse was still in the field), physicing the wretched animal and 'mashing him down' for several days is thankfully rarely used now, at least not in up-to-date yards who absorb the fruits of the considerable equine research carried out over the last ten or twenty years. This practice went completely against one of the golden rules of feeding: make no sudden changes in feed. Grass was removed altogether, a totally unnecessary and harsh laxative was given which had a severe and damaging purging effect on the animal (with a view to 'clearing the grass out of his system') and bran was suddenly introduced. Bran itself is quite an indigestible food, contrary to what is still popularly believed. So apart from having his natural food, grass – which the microbes in the horse's gut were attuned to coping with – suddenly removed, the purging physic was administered, killing off many of the microbes anyway and causing severe and intentional diarrhoea; then indigestible and unappetising bran mashes were offered, which continued the purging effect since there were few microbes able to cope with them.

All this had a very lowering effect on the horse (at a time when his connections were intending to build him up and get him fit!) and it was very common for him to go back significantly in condition. This was a complete waste of time and money. It could take several weeks for the horse to recover fully from this treatment and regain not only his strength but his digestive capabilities.

How much more economical and effective to begin working the horse from the field and give him a small 'hard' feed on return, so gradually accustoming the gut microbes to a change of food and allowing those involved in the digestion of the new food to multiply. In the early stages, there isn't even any need to get the horse shod; he can do his walking in his field or on soft tracks if there are any, and short trips on hard *smooth* roads will not harm him at all provided his feet are professionally trimmed and balanced. This saves on shoeing, bedding and grooming. It also avoids the lost days and weeks which the horse would spend recovering from the physic and mashing down.

The same basic principles apply whether the fitness programme is starting in spring, summer, autumn or winter. Seasonal considerations do apply, of course, and in autumn or winter it may be easier to get the horse fit if he is clipped and given a New Zealand rug (depending on how thick his coat grows). In spring and summer, grass may have to be gradually restricted to effect a slimmer shape and allow for harder food to be fed – although many showing and dressage competitors seem to be competing for the Fattest Horse prize rather than the prize for the best conformed or the most agile, correct performance! The penny has obviously not yet dropped, in some circles, that obesity is not only ugly and damaging to health and performance but is also expensive to maintain.

3 Money

There is very little you can do without money. Most people think they haven't got enough and very few admit to having too much. It is noticeable that those who grumble that their money gives them nothing but problems never seem to divest themselves of it in quantities sufficient to bring them down to the breadline! Money's advantages, it seems, definitely outweigh its disadvantages.

Unfortunately for us, horses come within the range of 'expensive tastes'. They are expensive animals to buy (yet not very profitable to sell unless you are producing world-class competition horses or bloodstock) and expensive to keep. There is nothing wrong with cutting costs in horse keeping (provided the horses do not suffer) and everything to be gained by sensible and prudent economies. It might even mean the difference between keeping one horse or two (maybe an outgrown pony to be turned to driving) or, indeed, keeping a horse at all.

Expenses can be cut drastically if you share a horse with someone else, although difficulties may arise over use and management. This is especially likely if you do not actually own a share in the horse but merely help pay the bills, and any sharing arrangement must be gone into very carefully, preferably with a written agreement on both sides.

For the amateur horse owner not out to actually earn a living from his or her horse, the only way to be financially prudent is to get and keep costs down and run the operation with a strict eye on the pounds and pence. True, competitions won can bring valued extra pounds into the kitty, but income from this source should be regarded as a bonus and not as an essential boost to the funds needed to keep the horse.

If you happen to be willing and able to give lessons to other people, either on your horse or on theirs, you are officially classed as a self-employed instructor and should declare this income on your annual tax return. Should you make a habit of it, you are best advised to do the job properly and consult an accountant about the various implications.

For a start, an accountant will inform you that there are certain expenses you can claim against your 'business', such as travelling to and from your clients, at least some of the maintenance of your horse (you will not be able to claim all his expenses as tax deductible against your business if the taxman construes that he was your private horse before you began instructing and that you still use him for enjoyment), some, again, of your own horse-related expenses such as your clothing and also transportation to shows which could be regarded as a publicity operation to keep you in the public eye and attract custom. A good accountant will save you in tax more than his fee, which is also tax deductible.

There are various advantages to being self-employed in that losses in the business can be set against past income from other sources (e.g. your main job, even though you may pay PAYE tax in connection with it) and against future profits. Tax is also paid a year in arrears and is normally due in two instalments. Unfortunately, you have to have the willpower to set aside regular amounts to cover it. An ordinary paid job, if you have one, or another profitable business will probably use up your personal allowance, so the whole of your net earnings from your instructing will be liable to whatever rate of tax you are on. In other words, if you are a basic-rate taxpayer, like most of the population, you will be taxed at that rate on what is left of your income after your expenses have been deducted.

If you collected £1000 in your first year of instructing, for instance, and your expenses amounted to £1050, you made a loss of £50 which, assuming you have another, main job, could mean a refund of £50 from the Inland Revenue – in due course. If, however, you collected £1000 and your expenses amounted to £750, you made a profit of £250 and will be taxed at your normal rate on £250.

You may also be liable to pay Class 2 (self-employed) insurance stamps every week if your net income (that is, your earnings less your expenses) rises above a certain level for the year. It is quite permissible to pay these stamps or contributions a year in arrears, because if you are new in the business and do not know what your net income is going to be, you will not know if you are, in fact, liable to pay them. The fact that you are already paying a Class 1 stamp as an employee makes no difference to your liability: the

Class 2 stamp is compulsory when your net income rises above a certain level.

The main bugbear is that for the Class 2 stamp you receive *no* extra benefits from the state. It is simply another form of tax. Even if you decide to go into business full time and give up your paid job, the benefits you receive from Class 2 contributions are very limited in comparison with a Class 1 contribution. Extra insurances such as permanent health insurance (to protect your income should you be ill or have an accident and be unable to earn), life assurance (to protect your dependants, if appropriate, in the event of your death) and a pension plan (to provide for your old age and give you a standard of living above the poverty line) are advisable. You will also need third party insurance, and professional indemnity insurance to cover you in the event of a claim against you for negligence or incompetence by one of your clients.

Some of these insurances are tax deductible and some are not. The whole scene of trying to make money out of your horse, or at least trying to make him pay for himself, is somewhat complicated, and if you are seriously considering trying it, you are strongly advised to consult an accountant. I also recommend that you buy two good books on the professional aspect of the horse business. The first is *Running a Stables as a Business* by Janet Macdonald (J. A. Allen) and the second title is *Horse Business Management* by Jeremy Houghton Brown and Vincent Powell-Smith (Blackwell Scientific Publications).

The 'small' horse owner is not normally advised to actually hire out his or her horse for 'hire or reward', in other words to let people pay for the pleasure of riding the horse without having instruction. This is construed as running a riding establishment and has a set of laws, rules and regulations of its own. Again, the above two books cover this if you are seriously thinking of making your living with horses. Another good move would be to put yourself on the British Horse Society Register of Instructors, which is possible provided you hold the society's minimum qualification of BHSAI (British Horse Society Assistant Instructor) or a higher BHS qualification in instructing.

The Truth, the Whole Truth and Nothing but the Truth!

Before you start a wholesale cost-cutting operation, it is sensible to find out exactly, and truthfully, how much your horse is costing you to keep now, over a period of a full year. Costs do vary according to the season. Many horses cost more to keep in winter because of the extra food needed in inclement weather – particularly working owners' horses who are out all day for exercise while their owners are at work. On the other hand, if you compete mostly in summer, your feed costs could be almost as high as in winter and you will also have the extra costs incurred in show entries, transportation to show grounds, perhaps desirable though not essential new items of tack and clothing for yourself to bring or keep your turnout up to desired standard, and so on.

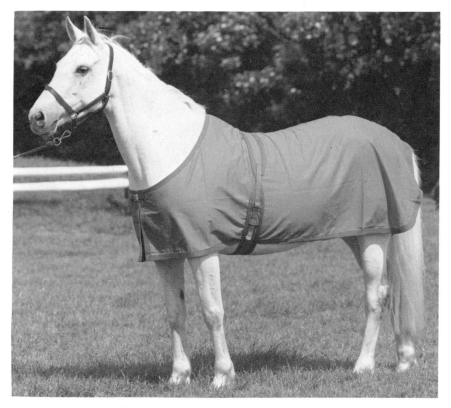

Fig. 5 Sew-it-yourself! One way to save money on clothing is to buy a ready cut-out kit from Acorn Rugs of Gairsheild Farm, Steel, Hexham, Northumberland. This photo shows their summer sheet. Other kits are also available, in quilted fabrics and with crossed rather than conventional surcingles. The patterns are shaped along the spine seam to follow the shape of the horse's back and represent excellent value for money, normally offering a saving of a third or more off normal prices (see Table 3.1).

You may well say: 'I don't care how much he costs. He's my hobby and my pride and joy and I work hard to have him. I'll gladly pay out to keep him.' I know the feeling, but that's no reason why you shouldn't avoid paying out unnecessarily. Most of us have felt the pinch at some time, have wanted a super-quality rug but could only afford a medium-quality one, have blenched at an emergency vet's bill or grumbled at the price of hay. No successful business runs on a 'money-is-no-object' basis, and the more careful you are with what money you have, the more you can get for it and do with it. If you consider that keeping a competition horse at home, where you have no livery charges, can easily cost you £3,000 a year if you compete at all seriously, and compare that with, say, roughly half that or less for a weekend hack kept also at home, you can see the desirability of watching every pound. If those horses are at livery or simply in rented accommodation your costs can shoot up considerably.

Eking your money out is not mean – it is sensible. Indeed, it may mean the difference between having enough put aside to afford that emergency vet's bill, or delaying calling the vet because the thought of the bill frightens you and then ending up with a seriously ill horse on your hands. Apart from the suffering caused to the horse, such a situation will almost surely cost you more in the end than calling the vet in the early stages.

So, then, sit down with a piece of paper and a pen when you have time to concentrate and do the job properly, and write down absolutely everything from the past year that you can remember. Even if you have not kept your feed bills, you will have a fairly accurate idea of how much your average bill is for the foodstuff you buy. You know how much you pay your farrier for a new set or pair of shoes, for a remove or a trim. You know how much your rent or livery is, if applicable. Also, write down every little item of tack you bought over the year – that swish new browband that created a judge's-eye-catching contrast with your horse's coat colour, that new bit you tried but discarded, and your own clothing, including such seemingly insignificant items such as hairnets or thermal insoles for your boots!

Repairs should go down, from a major re-stuffing of your saddle to a tiny rip in your New Zealand rug or a single stirrup leather that needed re-stitching. To be fair, you should also list postal expenses (for paying bills and sending off show entries), peppermints and other specially purchased tit-bits for your horse, instruction fees, travelling expenses to and from the stables if your horse is not at home, and everything like that. Otherwise, you are not telling yourself the truth.

If you want to do things the accountant's way, you should work out how much your horse and all his and your equipment, taking into account its depreciation, are worth and enquire how much interest you would have earned in a year in, say, a high-yielding building society account on that amount of capital. If your premises are at home, ask how much less Council Tax you would have to pay if you had no stables, fodder storage facilities or paddocks, and add that to the calculations.

When you have listed absolutely all your expenses, add them up and divide them by twelve or fifty-two to arrive at the monthly or weekly amount your equestrian activities are costing you. If you haven't fallen over in a faint, you can make things look slightly better by taking off that total the amounts of any winnings or earnings you have accrued. Then, to be cruel to yourself again, imagine how much interest your yearly expenditure *plus* the capital value of horse, etc. would have earned if you had invested it in the aforementioned building society account – an interesting evening's doodling, to show just how expensive horses *really* are to keep! To be serious, of course, one of the uses of money is to bring pleasure and if your horse is something you cannot live without this is money well spent. Looking at it that way, the more you save on expenses the more pleasure you can get from it! At least, you will be able comfortably to put some by for a critical time in your horsy activities, such as an unexpected illness or accident, instead of operating on a hand-to-mouth basis every week or month. Having worked out the true actual costs of keeping a horse might just make you realise how desirable it is to keep a tight rein on them (no pun intended).

Your Budget

Budgets are things which no business can run without, unless it is extremely fortunate. Most other operations, from households to private individuals – in other words things which are not normally regarded as businesses – also run to a budget, even though they may not realise it. You have to cut your coat according to your cloth, whatever your circumstances.

A budget is really just a money timetable, and timetables are an excellent way of ensuring that, as far as possible, things run according to plan. (Schools, for instance, would be chaos without a timetable. So would public transport systems and any business or other operation which runs on an appointment or consulting period/surgery system, such as dentists, doctors, veterinary practices, advisory services and the like.)

It will be quite simple to work out a budget for yourself, having done the totting up described in the preceding paragraphs. Even if you have no business experience, you may have heard of something called a cash flow statement or cash flow forecast. This is simply a crystal ball operation, whereby a business person makes estimates (glorified guesses) as to how much money he or she will be spending on a certain item in a certain month. Then, if wise, he or she will make sure that the money needed to pay those expenses is available at the time required, either from what the business earns, from bank loans or overdrafts or from an injection of personal capital (i.e. personal money being put into the business) if strictly necessary.

The amateur horse owner will need to operate in a very similar way by allocating money regularly from salary or other income to make sure his or her money timetable/budget/cash flow forecast (all the same thing) is running to schedule.

First you will need a large sheet of paper (say, two sheets of A4 taped together down the middle). It should be ruled across with a top line for the months of the year, a bottom line for totals and as many other lines in between as you have categories plus a few more for forgotten items or new ones that crop up as you go along.

Next, rule it vertically so that you end up with twenty-six columns for figures and a wider column down the left-hand side for you to name the items the figures relate to, e.g. livery, shoeing, vetcrinary expenses, transport, etc. At the head of the figure columns put 'January' over the first two, 'February' over the next two and so on to the end of the year. Over the two final columns on the right-hand side put 'totals'. You now have your empty budget sheet, ready and waiting for your figures (see Table 3.1).

You have, from your previous calculations, the figures you spent on each category over the previous twelve months, but inflation is still with us so here you must make a reasoned guess at what inflation is going to be over the forthcoming twelve months. If you think it will be 5%, multiply all your individual category totals

	January		February		March		April		May		June		July		August		September		October		November		December		TOTAL	
	Budget	Actual	Budget	Actual	Budget	Actual	Budget	Actual	Budget	Actual	Budget	Actual	Budget	Actual	Budget	Actual	Budget	Actual	Budget	Actual	Budget	Actual	Budget	Actual	Budget	Actual
Livery																										
Rent																										
Feed																										
Bedding																										
Farriery																										
Veterinary																										
Instruction																										
Horse box/trailer maintenance																										
Petrol/diesel/oil																										
Tack (inc. repairs)																										
Horse clothing																										
Rider clothing																										
Entry fees																										
Postage																										
Premises maintenance																										
Land care and maintenance																										
Hire of facilities (jumps, manege)																										
Subscriptions																										
Registration fees																										
Sundries																										
TOTAL																										

Table 3.1 *Sample basic budget layout*

(livery, shoeing, etc.) by 5% to give you a probable figure for the forthcoming year.

Do not, however, then divide your estimate equally by twelve to give a monthly figure as some figures will vary according to the season. Your livery or rent charge may be the same all year round but transport may not be if, for instance, you don't compete in winter. Here you have to use your common sense, based on last year's actual events (and bills/receipts, if you have kept them) and, within your total, allocate a reasonable amount for that particular expense to each month.

When you have done that, put your expected figure (your budget or forecast figure) in the first (left-hand) column under each month. Do this for every item, every month. Then total up each month and write in the figure in the relevant space on the 'total' line which runs along the bottom of your sheet. Next, tot up your categories across the columns and put each category total in the first of the two total columns running down the right-hand side of your sheet.

In the bottom right-hand corner you will have two blank total spaces. Add up all the totals along the bottom line (whatever did we do before home calculators were invented?) and pencil in the figure you get in the left-hand space. Now add up all the totals in the column you have filled in down the right-hand side of the sheet and see what your calculator says. It *should* say the same as the figure you have already pencilled in. If it does, it is said to 'balance'. Assuming it does, ink it over and you have completed your budget.

You will notice, however, that you have just as many columns left blank as are filled in. This is so that you can fill in your monthly expenditure for each category as you go along, and put the appropriate monthly total actually spent (known sensibly enough as the 'actual' figure) on the right of your 'budget' or 'forecast' figure. This enables you to see how you are doing as the year progresses. If your actuals are regularly more than your budgets, you've got a problem. Either your sums were wrong in the first place or inflation is significantly more than you expected or your costs have risen quite unexpectedly (livery stable changed hands and put charges up, for example) or your calculator batteries were running down!

At least you can see in black and white what is happening and will be warned in plenty of time that you are going to overspend if things carry on as they are. This can warn you to make economies in other areas or to allocate more money from your income if you want to avoid getting into trouble.

Should you be fortunate enough to be accumulating a surplus instead of a deficit you may, if you wish (you are the chairman of this particular company, after all), go on a spending spree and buy a new saddle or a luxurious all-wool day rug with your family coat of arms on it. On the other hand, if you were intending to buy a new saddle and/or day rug anyway, but omitted to put the relevant cost into your budget, their subsequent purchase could play havoc with your money timetable and you will almost certainly show a deficit at the end of the year.

That is basically how a budget works, and if you have never used one before you could be amazed what a tempering effect it has on your spending urges. It also gives you a self-satisfied glow when you see everything running according to plan, with your actuals very near your budgets. Should your end-of-year forecast totals come within 1% of your actual totals, apply to the Treasury for a job – your country needs you!

Before you dash off to prepare your cash flow forecast, there is one more thing. It is a very wise step to set up for yourself a thing called a 'contingency fund' or 'emergency fund'. As its name implies, this is a reserve fund to fall back on in unexpected, dire circumstances (you have a fall and your saddle tree is broken, your trailer sustains four punctures due to animal rights activists scattering tacks in the road, a gale whips the roof off your hay store and, for some strange reason, your insurance policy does not cover it, etc., etc., etc.). This contingency fund can be as big or as small as you like (or as your finances permit), but there should be one of some kind. Perhaps an additional 10% on top of your yearly forecast figure would be adequate and reasonable? Well, maybe 7.5% – but *something*, anyway.

Where to Put Your Money

Banks and other financial institutions tell us that there are still millions of Britons who do not have a bank account of any kind. One reason for not having one seems to be: 'I like to keep my money affairs to myself.' Another, more recent reason is: 'They put all their information about you on computer where anybody can get at it.' A slight exaggeration, perhaps, but not unfounded.

Yet another reason is: 'It's not worth it; there'd never be enough in my account to be worth their while – in fact, they'd charge me for the privilege.'

One can understand the reasoning behind all these statements and they all possess an element of truth. Let us consider, however, some good reasons for having a bank account.

For a start, it can be very convenient. Whenever you write out a cheque you have an instant receipt and proof of payment for the item concerned. Even if you forget to fill in the cheque stub, your bank can confirm whether or not any cheque you query has been cashed. Then when your feed merchant keeps sending you nasty letters about an allegedly unpaid bill you can throw unassailable proof in his face.

If you lose your cheque book it is useless to anyone who finds it (or has stolen it) because he will not have your cheque guarantee card to enable him to forge your signature, and no sensible trader these days will accept a cheque without a cheque card except from someone he knows and deals with regularly. Banks always advise us not to keep our card and book together because separately they are useless. If they are together, however, the finder/thief is on to a good thing for a limited length of time. If you inform the bank of your loss immediately you discover it, your liability is very limited no matter how much has been withdrawn from the account.

If, on the other hand, you lose cash you will be extremely lucky to get it back.

Having a bank account, and a record of your in-payments (by filling in the stubs in your paying-in book or the paying-in stubs which are found at the back of some cheque books) and your drawings or out-payments (by filling in the cheque stubs), you will find it quite easy to keep track of your money. If you take the trouble to fill in all stubs with the date, the name of the payee (the person you are paying), what the payment was for and the invoice (bill) number, if appropriate, together with the amount, and if you keep a running balance (taking off and adding on all amounts you pay in and pay out as you go along in the spaces provided for this on the cheque stubs), you have a ready-made record always to hand.

I find it a good idea to write on the back of the cheque itself what the payment was for, again adding an invoice number if there is one. Then, if you lose your stubs once the book is empty, you can always ask the bank to trace the cheque and the information will be there on the back ready for you. (Most banks do not any longer return cheques to account holders automatically, but they do keep them themselves for about three years.) If you want to be really careful, write on the invoice the number of the cheque with which you paid it – then it won't take you more than a few seconds to confirm, from the statement of your account which the bank will send you regularly, whether and when payment was made.

If you want to pay everything in cash you run into various inconveniences. Delivery men are often not authorised to accept payments but will instead give you a delivery note stating what has been delivered: you sign two copies of the note, they take one back and you keep one (which should be matched or 'reconciled' with the invoice related to that order). You can send cash through the post, of course, but the post office prefer you to send it by Registered Post which is quite expensive. You are not supposed to send money by Recorded Delivery, and if you do you will not receive compensation if it is lost en route. With Registered Post compensation is payable, but the much cheaper Recorded Delivery service only enables you to trace proof of delivery. In any event, both services mean a trip to the post office.

These factors could easily lead you to waste time and transport expenses going to pay bills in person. Postal orders can be sent by post, of course, but they cost money and you have to remember to keep the stubs if you want to trace whether or not they have been cashed. You can pay by bank giro or by the post office's Transcash system, but there will usually be a charge for this and, again, it involves a trip to the bank or post office.

Bank charges are not, at the time of writing, charged by most high street banks or by National Girobank, even if you do not have a minimum amount (such as £50 or £100) in your account. Charges, or rather interest, does loom, however, if you overdraw (write cheques totalling more than you have in your account), with or without permission. (The bank cannot 'bounce', i.e. refuse to pay out on, your cheques if you write your cheque guarantee card number on the back. Your payees will require this as it protects them from 'rubber cheques', but if you do it and have not enough money in your account, *and do not have permission to overdraw in the form of an overdraft*, you will be in hot water with the bank and will probably have your guarantee card taken away.)

Most banks and building societies now offer interest, albeit low, on current or cheque accounts but, at the time of writing, you don't usually automatically get one of these accounts unless you ask for one. Another useful facility often offered as a package with an interest-bearing current account is a small free overdraft (in other words no interest is charged on the first named amount, such as £100). This facility is automatic and you do not have to ask to overdraw to this amount. This facility might be extended, for example, to an automatic overdraft of, say, £1,000 on which you only pay interest on the last £900. Again, you don't have to ask permission to overdraw and this can be very useful if your income is erratic or you have had a lot of expenses lately. It can be cheaper than using your credit card, depending on exact conditions. There is no free credit period with an automatic overdraft (excluding the initial free amount if this applies) so if you can be sure you can make up the overdrawn amount within the free credit period offered by your credit card company, you would obviously find it cheaper to use the card rather than the overdraft.

Even a savings-type account such as a bank deposit account, a building society account (without cheque book) or a post office account of some kind, is better than stuffing your money in jamjars around the house or keeping it under the mattress. It will be safe, you will be given a book in which all the transactions (ins and outs) on your account are recorded, so again you will know just where you are. An account of this kind will also earn you some interest on your money. Because the money is safely put away, the temptation of dipping into it is largely removed too.

If you are a basic-rate taxpayer is it best to open a building society or a bank deposit account as well as a current account. These pay more interest than the interest-bearing current/cheque accounts at present, sometimes considerably more if you leave over a certain amount in them, calculated on a rising scale in increments, usually, of a few thousand pounds. These accounts are, at present, subject to basic rate tax which means tax on your interest is deducted at the current basic rate before you get it, but you *can* claim it back (consult your bank manager or accountant) if you are not a taxpayer.

The Post Office also have various accounts suitable for taxpayers and non-taxpayers and if you prefer this organisation by all means put your money there. Its opening hours may be more convenient for you although many banks now open virtually normal office hours, but still not on Saturday mornings which is where the Post Office can score for working horse owners who wish to make personal visits to the source of their money rather than doing everything by automatic transfers and cheques etc.

Whatever sort of account you open other than a current/cheque account, check how quickly you can get at your money. Some tie up your money for three months and pay you a higher rate of interest than those which only tie it up for a month, a week or not at all. If you are only happy with 'instant access', i.e. you want to be able to walk into the branch or office and get your money on the spot, make this quite clear when you enquire about the various accounts so that you do not get any nasty shocks later and end up with a sheaf of bills you cannot pay for several weeks and a mob of angry creditors. If you get a reputation for late payment, even if it *is* due to a misunderstanding, you will find their services hard to procure in the future. Most banks and building societies allow you instant access to your money anyway but you lose the interest on the amount you withdraw, which I feel is a minor penalty for remaining in your suppliers' good books.

Having opened your account, of whatever kind, you must steel yourself to pay into it every week or month (depending on how you receive your income) whatever amount your budget sheet tells you you are going to need that month to keep your horse. If you have a job, firms are willing and able to pay your wages or salary (either all or part of it, as you prefer) directly into a bank account or sometimes a building society account. If your income is from an investment source, you should again be able to have the money paid directly into an account. Be warned, however, that it is not always – or indeed usually – possible to have your money paid directly into a *deposit* bank account or a post office account, although this situation might change in the future.

If you have a personal current/cheque account at a bank, it is a simple matter to open a special 'horse account' and have a regular automatic transfer made from your personal account to your horse account by means of a standing order (a payment from the personal account into the Horse Account on prearranged dates, such as the first day of every month). However, if your budget shows differing amounts each month and you prefer to stick to the monthly/seasonal variations exactly, a standing order will not do because if you keep changing the amount of your standing order you will soon become unpopular with the bank and may be charged. You will simply have to pay the relevant amounts in yourself, by cheque from your personal account or just by signing a transfer form at the bank.

There is another type of cheque/current account which can be helpful if you think you are going to be operating near the edge of the cliff – in other words, if you think you are going to need more money for your horse than you have put by or have ready to hand in your personal account. This is called a budget account, and most high street banks operate them. You simply pay in (usually by standing order from your personal account) the same amount every month. Then, if you need to pay out more than you have in your budget account you can, because the bank lets you overdraw. Show your bank manager your expertly prepared cash flow forecast/budget. This will assure him that you know what you are doing as far as money is concerned, that you have a responsible attitude to it and that, by the end of the year, the situation will almost certainly have resolved itself. There is an interest charge on overdrawn budget accounts, but the cost is small compared to the convenience.

If you have budgeted carefully, however, and allowed for a contingency/emergency fund, you should find that your horse account builds up gradually over the year. This means there will be extra cash in a current account not earning high interest, and you should transfer the surplus into one of the higher interest-bearing accounts mentioned above. Then you won't have to pay for your horse's Polo Mints, Mars Bars or whatever it is he likes out of your carefully put-aside horse money – the interest from your bank or building society will pay for them!

How to Avoid Spending Money

Having discussed a suitable home for your money and methods of money management, let's think about ways of not spending it.

If, like most people, you have to keep your horse away from home, your biggest expense will be livery charges. This is usually an all-in charge covering rent of stable and grazing, labour for the horse to be looked after and exercised, and the costs of his feed and bedding.

In many areas of the country, particularly those near or actually in towns and cities, good livery premises and services are *extremely* hard to get. The most popular areas are on the outskirts of the urban areas or just into the rural parts. These areas are reasonably easily accessible for owners and are usually near fair riding facilities (not many livery owners would be content with riding round and round an indoor school or manège or even round the same few fields all the time), offering commuters or city dwellers a chance to enjoy their horses in the countryside or at least away from the city's noise and fumes. Establishments sited actually in urban areas are normally near parks which offer riding facilities.

The livery proprietor obviously bases his or her charges on the yard's overheads, and business rates play a large part in this. Owners might, therefore, expect to pay more for livery in an urban establishment than in a semi-rural one, all else being equal. As discussed in chapter 1, the best guide to choosing a good establishment is the condition of the horses and ponies already in residence, although you would of course also be far happier if you were at a yard where you liked the proprietor and staff. Although we are currently thinking of how to *save* money, it might be better to spend a bit extra to be sure of a good place and have the peace of mind this brings, rather than penny-pinch and be worrying about your horse's welfare all the time.

If, like many people, you do not have much choice as to the actual yard you use, livery being hard to come by in your chosen area, consider ways in which you might be able to pay a little less without compromising on your horse's care. For instance, your yard might charge more for stabling your horse in a brick box than a wooden one because of the higher initial building/erection costs. It is lovely to have a brick box, of course, provided its location is as attractive for the horse as others, i.e. he can see out easily and watch what is going on in the yard and feel part of things, if that is what he prefers, or conversely he can be quiet and peaceful if that suits him better; but if the livery charge is stretching your bank balance somewhat (or even if it isn't) and there is a wooden box which would do the job just as well for a few pounds a week less, why not have that one instead? Similarly, if your charge includes use of show jumps and cross-country course but you and your horse never jump a stick, why not try to negotiate a reduction in your payment?

This might be construed by some as nit-picking; I prefer to call it avoidance of waste (why pay for something you don't want?) or economising. It may be that you have to pay a flat fee for everything whether you like it or not, but there is no harm in asking. As regards the services offered, some yards do charge a flat fee but others only charge you for what you actually want. For instance, if your horse is not being turned out to graze for some reason – perhaps because he is ill – you should not be charged for the use of the field during that period. If he *is* ill and is not being exercised, you should not be charged for exercising either. Although the yard proprietor may claim that a sick horse takes up as much time in nursing as a healthy one takes in other respects, this is not normally true. Grooming, for example, takes a good half-hour a day, but no sick horse should be subjected to a thorough grooming and strapping every day – he would be much better off left in peace and messed about as little as possible, short of being made to feel alone and neglected.

You will be governed largely by the yard's pricing policy, but there are ways of economising on livery charges if you think about, and preferably discuss with the proprietor, the possibilities of economising before you move your horse in. If the yard produces an itemised list of services and appropriate charges from which you can pick and choose, by all means take advantage of it; but if not, be sure to find out whether different stables are charged at different rates and exactly what facilities and services are thrown in (e.g. use of prepared riding areas, use of jumps, tack cleaning, laundering of rugs, use of horse-walker, etc.) so that you can negotiate terms appropriate to your requirements.

If you do have a choice of yards which would meet your requirements as regards looking after your horse, it may be worth foregoing the indoor school and/or outdoor manège, the automatic waterer in the box and the cross-country course you do not need – not to mention the brick box just discussed – and opting for the cheaper, less impressive establishment which will still ensure your horse's well-being and happiness, especially if it is a bit nearer your home and therefore quicker and cheaper to get to.

You will not normally be bothered with equipment, feed and bedding costs and the like in minute detail if you keep your horse at livery. However, if you are responsible for these yourself, because your horse is either at home or in a do-it-yourself livery situation, you will soon become cost conscious and will be on the lookout for ways to cut down costs in these areas.

It usually pays to get good-quality equipment of whatever sort because of its longer wearing qualities and superior in-use benefits. This applies to tack and clothing as well as equipment like mucking-out tools, grooming kit, buckets and so on.

You may consider acquiring certain expensive items like

tack, harness and New Zealand rugs second hand, and this is quite feasible as long as you know what to look for (no cracked, stiff leather or worn, rotten stitching). Second-hand, good quality equipment and tack is far preferable to brand-new, poorer quality stuff. Tack is often available at saddlers, and if you go to a firm which is a member of the Society of Master Saddlers (evidenced by the society's distinctive oval crest on its stationery, catalogues and, perhaps, displayed on the premises) you can be sure of having access to expert advice. And anyway, no reputable firm would stock shoddy, poor-quality tack, whether new or second hand.

Other equipment, such as barrows, corn bins, brooms, shovels, and so on, can often be bought at farm sales, in particular, or occasionally at sales where riding establishments or other agriculture-based enterprises are closing down. The classified advertisements in your local farming press or regional equestrian publication (if you have one) might also reveal bargains in such goods, but don't make the mistake of spending pounds in petrol or diesel, or paying heavy transportation charges to get your haul back to base. You could end up having spent as much as you would have done if you had bought new nearer home.

If you keep your horse in company with other owners at a yard where you do your horses yourselves and are responsible for finding all your own equipment, there are various ways in which you can save some cash.

An excellent scheme I once experienced is for all the owners to join in a 'kitty budget', each owner paying an identical amount per horse owned to a separate fund each week or month to buy a communally owned pool of equipment such as mucking-out tools, cheap headcollars for leading to and from the field, a third-hand harrow for the paddocks and so on. (The social aspects of operating like this are discussed in the next chapter, but basically it *can* work very well in practice.)

If there are, say, eight owners in the yard, it is unlikely that all eight will be present and mucking out at exactly the same time, so there is no point in each owner buying a full set of mucking-out tools. Instead, two or three could be purchased from the fund. The most expensive item of mucking-out equipment will be the barrow. However, a barrow is not essential. Polyethylene mucksheets, circular in shape with a drawstring round the outside, can be laid outside the box door and the muck shovelled on to them. Then, the drawstring can be pulled tight and the 'sack' heaved off to the manure heap over your shoulder – if you have the strength. An even cheaper alternative is to open out a feed sack – again polyethylene, which seems to have almost universally replaced hessian (paper and plastic are obviously useless for our purpose) – pile the muck on and simply gather up the four corners to contain the muck. This is not quite so effective and you will probably lose some out of the sides, but it is certainly very economical.

A most useful item of equipment is a muck skip or skep, so that you can regularly (when you are present) remove droppings and avoid any more soiling of bedding than is absolutely essential. Saddlers and stable equipment shops sell these, but there is no need to buy one. Old dustbin lids make quite adequate skips or, if you have a plastic mesh laundry bin for storing your roots, the lid from that will do (provided you don't also use it on the root bin!). Still on the subject of laundry and bedding, a household laundry basket makes a good skep, too.

A few communal headcollars could also be purchased from the fund, four being adequate for eight horses and owners. You will all want your own for such things as attending shows, transportation, tying up in the box and so on, but having a pool of cheap ones takes some of the wear and tear away from your best ones. If any horse has to have a headcollar left on in the field because he is hard to catch, it is safer to use an old leather one for this as it will break under strain should the horse get caught in a hedge or catch his hind foot in the headcollar when scratching his ear. (This can happen even with well-fitting headcollars.) Nylon headcollars are cheap but very strong and are not, therefore, suitable for field use.

The kitty budget can be regularly boosted by putting into it the money from the sale of the yard's manure, probably to nurseries or private individuals (or perhaps you might be interested in going into business producing and selling your own mushrooms!).

With the other owners at your yard, you are in a position to take advantage of bulk purchase prices of bedding, feedstuffs, professional contract transport to shows, veterinary supplies (such as worming medicines) and services such as annual or six-monthly check-ups, teeth checks, vaccinations, etc. and farriery services. Vets and farriers are very busy people who do not charge travelling time and expenses for fun – they would rather do several horses on one visit than waste time tripping backwards and forwards, time they could use for other calls. As a commune, you split one visit fee between you. Similarly with freeze marking, an essential

Figs 6 and 7 A good New Zealand rug can be a real boon to a working owner who wishes to be able to leave his or her horse out on long winter days during working hours. This one, by the Greenham Saddlery Company of Ridge House, Greenham, Wellington, Somerset, has all the properties of a quality product, with shaping to fit the horse so that the rug is 'self-righting' in action, a drawstring round the quarters and a tail flap to ward off the worst of the weather when the horses stand, as they do, with their tails to the wind.

security precaution today in my view. It costs less per horse if several horses are done together than if the operator has to make a special visit for one horse.

To enjoy, as an individual, significant savings on feed and bedding, each owner in the yard works out how much hay (or whatever commodity is being purchased) his or her horse will need over a given period; then all the owners' figures are added together and a quotation obtained from a merchant or farmer for that quantity. When the invoice arrives, each owner pays his or her portion of the cost, so buying only what he or she needs but enjoying the lower bulk price.

If your do-it-yourself yard has a manager (probably the owner of the premises), he or she could be delegated to manage the kitty budget and bulk purchase arrangements. If this is not feasible, you will need to elect from among you a responsible individual to take on the job and keep proper, if simple, records of who has paid what and when – but hopefully this shouldn't be too difficult.

As well as buying in bulk, there are other ways of economising on feeding without cutting down your horse's nutritional standard. Remember that many 'big name' cubes and coarse mixes are more expensive and no better than others made locally or regionally by lesser-known firms. The analysis will be on the bags of all reputable makes, so if you don't understand it (and few of we ordinary mortals do) note down the details and check with your vet or an equine nutritionist whether it is suitable and recommended.

Feed supplements, too, can be very expensive, so check whether there is a cheaper one which would do your job just as well or whether, in fact, you need a supplement at all.

Your horse or pony will, of course, eat more if he feels cold, so do take advantage of the excellent modern range of horse clothing now available to insulate him against cold and wet. If he is stabled, his box should be well ventilated without there being any gaps between boards or under the door. Many people sweep the bedding away from behind the door to prevent the horse 'walking' it out with him but, for warmth, I prefer to actually bank it up there. It protects against draughts and also gives the horse something soft to stand on when he is in.

The less of his coat you clip off the less he will feel the cold, obviously. If you are doing light work it is worth considering if you could use a less extensive clip than you were perhaps thinking of.

Only horses with very thick, greasy coats really need a full or hunter clip. Horses with any 'blood' in them at all could manage perfectly well in fast work with a blanket clip which protects the vital back and loin areas. A glance at racing on television almost any winter afternoon will show you many racehorses either trace clipped or, more commonly, chaser clipped (a trace clip with the head hair removed also); if they can be made racing fit with such a clip, it is surely suitable for the rest of us.

Note, also, the racehorses' tails. Most of them have full tails at the top with a neat, straight bang across the bottom. Full tails look lovely on horses provided they are well kept; they can always be plaited for special occasions and then look much more attractive than pulled tails, to me anyway. The most important point is that the full dock hair protects your horse's vulnerable buttocks region against cold winds. Horses always stand with their tails to the wind, and studies in America with very similar groups of horses kept under identical conditions show that those with pulled tails lost 20% more condition during a winter living out than did those with natural full tails. So the moral is obvious.

Waste in feeding is also expensive. Galvanised bins or hoppers not only keep your feed in good shape but are vermin proof, which sacks are not. Plastic dustbins make a fair substitute (although determined rats have been known to chew through them) but make sure the lids cannot be knocked off by horses accidentally gaining access to the feed room. Not only might the whole bin go over but the horse might be very ill as a result of over eating. If a line of bins the same height is neatly aligned, a pole can be passed through the handles on all the lids and fastened to the feed room wall or partition in the same way as slip rails are fastened across a gateway – into a holder with a drop-down block of wood to prevent a horse lifting it out.

Always check with the manufacturer of a proprietary feed how long it is supposed to keep and under what conditions, and do not buy more than you can use in that period as the rest will only 'go off' and be wasted. This particularly applies to feed supplements; it is no use buying the large economy size if it will not keep long enough for you to use it up.

Hay is subjected to a great deal of abuse in storage. How often do we see open-sided barns full of hay, and straw come to that, exposed to all weathers? Rain ruins the outer bales, and a leaky barn roof can quickly ruin the rest. Hay should ideally be kept in dry, well-ventilated buildings away from the weather. If it has to be kept outside due to lack of storage, it should be kept up off the ground or on a tough polythene groundsheet and covered, at least over the top, by a tarpaulin or more polythene. Buying these materials is cheaper than letting the hay go rotten. Try to stack the hay against a wall or something that will protect it from driving rain and the prevailing wind so that your covering is not easily blown away. Tie it down, too (perhaps with a home-made net made of baler twine), or weight it down with old tyres.

The cheapest time to buy hay and straw is off the field at harvest time, or even before if you can be certain it will be well made by your supplier. Buying in bulk at this time, even if you have to borrow money from your bank and pay interest on the loan or overdraft, is cheaper than buying the hay in small amounts as you need it, as you could easily be paying 50 or even 100% more by spring, particularly in a bad year. Remember that hay-age products are also made from the same thing – grass – so you are not automatically protected from price rises by turning to that instead.

If hay/hay-age prices are really getting ridiculous in any particular year, there are various alternatives which you can feed and still give your horse a good diet. Oat straw is one: good oat straw is more nutritious on its own than poor hay, particularly if the latter is dusty or mouldy. You will need to up the protein content of the rest of the diet, but a short consultation with a vet or equine nutritionist will soon sort out a suitable all-round diet.

If you like feeding individual grain feeds (oats, barley) rather than coarse mixes or cubes, do not buy more ready-crushed feed than you can use in a fortnight. Certainly within two to three weeks the grain, having had its kernel crushed and therefore killed, will begin to rot, like all dead things, and will be unfit to feed. Whole grain bought in bulk is not without its problems as it has to be stored at the correct temperature and humidity or it will begin to sprout, and most one or two-horse owners haven't got the necessary facilities. If you can go along to someone who has and buy moderate quantities as and when you want them, this could work well, but don't be tempted to buy large amounts if you haven't got proper storage.

In warm conditions, things like molasses meal or molassed chop or sugar beet pulp ferment very quickly and become unfit to feed, so in warm weather, if you want to give your horse the taste of molasses, buy tins of black treacle and keep them in a cool place, then dilute the treacle with hot water to melt it and use that to damp feeds or chop, if you wish.

Bran has for the past decade or more been an expensive feed, and it is one which most horses can do very well without. It is over rated as a feed and, indeed, too much in the diet can cause serious imbalance of the calcium:phosphorus ratio, so favouring bone disease. Chop is a safer substitute for adding bulk to feeds and, if you wish to feed your horse a mash, dried grass meal mixed with soaked sugar beet pulp is very acceptable to horses and nutritionally sound.

You should think very carefully before being diverted from a good basic diet, particularly if it has been formulated for you by an expert, just because you have heard of some fancy new feed or additive or supplement which is said to get a horse into tip-top condition and give him bags more energy than he has ever had before. Most of these feeds are expensive and unnecessary. Take advice before using them and work out carefully what the difference in cost to your budget will be. You may well find that you don't need them and can, in any case, get a cheaper alternative which will do the job just as well.

Roots such as carrots and swedes will be popular with your horse provided they are sound. Buying them from your grocer is most uneconomical, but buying stockfeed roots from a farm or merchant is much cheaper. Roots keep best in cool, dark, airy conditions, and keep better with the soil on than off. For 'small' horse owners, plastic mesh laundry bins are ideal storage containers. Remember to thoroughly rinse off the soil (and thus any chemicals it might contain) before feeding your horse, and only buy hard, crisp roots as any which have dark, soft or mouldy patches will quickly send the rest bad, too.

Waste is difficult to avoid with some horses; they throw their feed all over the place, trample it in the bedding or mud, blow it around and generally do anything but eat it. Apart from ensuring that your horse's teeth are in good condition and that he is properly de-wormed (so you are not feeding the worms as well), there are certain things you can do to control his manners at feedtime.

If feeding outdoors, haynets, although a bit time consuming to fill, keep hay under better control than anything else. Cattle racks do a reasonable job but are a hazard in the field where horses are concerned. The most wasteful way to feed hay is simply to tip it on the ground where it can be blown away or trodden into the mud. Feeding in racks or nets in the field shelter is the best solution (provided no horse is going to get chased away and forced to go without) as the hay is also kept dry. Feeding concentrates outdoors can also be tricky, unless someone is going to stand and hold each horse's container while he cleans up – which is rather time consuming. One way is to ram your bucket into an old car tyre so the horse cannot tip it up without some difficulty.

Feeding in the stable can be more easily controlled. Again, haynets are an economical way of feeding, but hayracks are good too, especially the large mesh type with a lid which (like the haynet) makes the horse take small quantities and prevents him pulling it all out over the top. A hay 'well' (as in old-fashioned stalls) often works as horses tend to stand over it and any hay dropped goes back into the well. These wells can easily be constructed by any competent handyman, but ask him to fit a pull-out tray on the bottom so you can clean it out easily. Indeed, the bits and seeds which remain on the bottom can usefully be added to your chop supply.

If your horse is a quiet eater, you can feed him from an ordinary bucket or even from a clean sack or piece of sheeting spread on the floor. However, if he scoops his feed out of his bucket or plain manger, or knocks containers over, get him a fixed manger in a triangular corner fitment, with bars over the corners which can be slid to one side by you to get the manger out for cleaning, but which the horse cannot manipulate. The bars prevent him from sliding his muzzle up the side and scooping the food out, and if the manger has an inward-turning lip the feed will simply fall back into it.

Saving on bedding is not simply a case of using the cheapest material you can get. For a start, your horse might need special dust-free bedding such as paper or the fabric bedding which has recently come on to the market, because of a respiratory allergy to the dust and spores often found in straw or a skin allergy to the chemicals often found in wood shavings and sawdust. In that case, you must of course use the product which keeps him in the best health, according to his problem. Also, not all materials may be readily available in your area so you may have to take what you can get.

Assuming you have a choice, obviously the thing to do is compare prices. Start with the one which appears to be the cheapest, then try them all in turn, keeping careful note of what it costs you for each material over an identical period of time under identical conditions.

Naturally, the less you use the less it will cost you, and in this connection deep litter bedding is certainly the cheapest system you can use. Details of managing this system are given in chapter 7. Basically, once the bed is established you need remarkably little material to keep it in good condition.

The enemies of any bed, obviously enough, are droppings and urine. If the horse never dirtied or wet his bed your problems would be over! It is certainly possible to 'house train' equines by teaching them to bang on their doors when they want to stale, but if a working owner's horse is stabled most of the day and there isn't anyone there to let him out, the object of the exercise is defeated and you could end up with a very worried horse!

A horse will normally pass about eight lots of droppings in twenty-four hours, and one of the secrets of successful bedding management (and therefore economy) is to remove them as soon as possible. Again, this is fine if someone is there to skip out stables fairly regularly, but is difficult otherwise.

You do, of course, save on bedding if your horse is out a good deal and, for those not using deep litter, a return to the old cavalry practice of laying bedding in a sheltered spot to dry out (tossing and turning it occasionally) might be considered. This idea only really works with straw; it would be virtually impossible to manage with shavings, sawdust or paper as they would blow all over the place.

The makers of paper bedding do, however, instruct users to turn and toss the bed to dry it out, for reasons of economy. This type of material is recommended to be used on a semi-deep litter basis (when it works very well). However, work undertaken by the Animal Health Trust indicates that, due to its super-absorbent qualities, it is not to be recommended for full deep litter as the amount of urine absorbed into the material can create problems in stables with even adequate ventilation.

Many working owners make economies of both time and labour on bedding by using semi-deep litter during the week, mucking out fully or nearly so at weekend. This, too, saves on material provided the bed is adequately managed. A bedding material made from flax and marketed under the name of Aubiose has recently been introduced and is proving popular with those who have tried it. It is flax chopped up small so makes a bed which looks rather like wood shavings but is finer. Unlike shavings, though, it seems to contain wetness in one place and to muck out you simply dig out the wet patches and remove droppings; the rest remains dry and just needs forking over to air it. It is best suited to semi-deep litter and deep litter beds. An added point in its favour is that it rots down more easily than shavings and is easier to dispose of to nurseries as muck. At 1992 prices, it cost about £40 to £50 to start off an Aubiose bed, but thereafter only half an £8.50 bale per week is needed for topping up. A reservation is that it is not suitable for horses which tend to dig in their beds as this distributes the moisture instead of containing it. It is claimed to be dust-free so can be recommended for horses with respiratory problems or those whose owners simply prefer a clean-air regime.

Stable floorings can go a long way to effect economy of material by helping to keep the bedding dry. Good stable floors achieve this by allowing urine to drain away from the bedding. Old books on management tell us that straw is a drainage bedding, its firm round stems shedding moisture and the old grooved stable-brick floors draining the urine away to a groove outside the boxes or behind stalls and thence to an inside or outside drain. Some boxes had (indeed, still have) central drains for the purpose actually inside the box. I am old enough (just) to remember straw like this and, although like many things it did not work in practice quite as well as in theory, it did drain urine away to a certain extent.

Unfortunately, today's straw is not at all like the old stuff. It is crushed and mangled up by harvesting methods and absorbs much more urine. Sawdust and shavings are absorbent, too; so is paper, and peat (an awful bedding material in my experience) can absorb up to nine times its own weight in moisture. However, it is the lower layers of a bed which naturally get the urine in the end so, at least with straw bedding, drainage flooring will help keep bedding somewhat drier.

Many modern stable floors are concrete, which is probably the worst material that could be used. Concrete itself absorbs moisture; it is also cold and hard. Even if grooved in a herringbone pattern ostensibly to take away the urine, this tends not to happen in practice, and the most bedding-saving floors are those which allow urine to drain through them.

Probably the best is loose-weave asphalt laid over gravel, over coarser gravel or rubble. The Irish National Stud experimented for

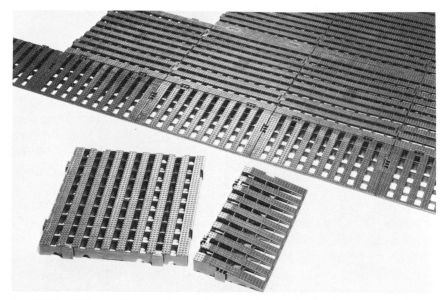

Fig. 8 The Ridry stable flooring system, proving 'fantastic' in use, according to users; the perforations allow urine to drain through and, especially if porous rubber matting (not metal reinforced) is laid on top, it enables quick, easy management with great savings in bedding and keeps the horse on a dry, warm, secure footing. The system works best, according to Mrs Janet Cross of Cobbacombe Farm, Huntsham, Tiverton, Devon, who markets the flooring, with long-shredded paper bedding, although others can be used.

some years with various different drainage floorings (including concrete slats and perforated concrete slabs over drains) and very much approved of the asphalt floor. They had drains under the gravel, but these are not strictly necessary. Asphalt itself is warm and softer, too, to the horse's feet and legs.

Another drainage flooring is ordinary house bricks (cheap from demolition sites) laid on gravel, or even earth, with a half-inch space all round between bricks. These floors in practice are hardwearing and allow urine to drain away in the cracks.

At present, a product new on the market is the Ridry Stable Flooring system which is described as 'a strong perforated platform which is laid under the bedding and allows moisture to pass through the straw. The horse, therefore, is always on a dry bed and only needs skipping out regularly.' The makers claim that the system can reduce the use of straw to as little as half a bale a week. The material costs about £25 per square metre but, taken medium term, the savings in bedding would be considerable.

This flooring system would work well on a grooved floor of any kind, or improve even more a drainage flooring such as the asphalt or brick ones mentioned. Care should be taken, however, to ensure that urine does not simply pool underneath it; the stable floor should, as ever, be slightly sloped towards some outlet if it is a non-drainage flooring like concrete. It would be pointless to use shavings or sawdust with the Ridry flooring system as in no time these materials would simply block it up.

The same company also make a porous rubber stable flooring; this comes in metre-square tiles which are not stuck down but can be moved around to give even wear and tear. There is no additional bedding used with these tiles and, at current rates, the company claim that purchasers will recoup bedding costs within three years. The tiles are guaranteed for five years and in practice should last much longer. It is maintained that, as horses are not nesting animals, they take to the flooring very quickly and lie and roll on it as normal, as it seems to them like the dry, bare earth patches they choose to lie on in nature, when given a choice. The Royal Veterinary College use the tiles and find them particularly useful for cases of colic when horses must not eat. Also, they cannot damage themselves so severely if thrashing about when coming round from a general anaesthetic as they are unable to get down to the concrete floor. Obviously, bedding costs and storage space are saved and a vast amount of time is saved in mucking out. Fuller details of the product and its applications and practical operation can be obtained from the company.

A simple earth floor, as used extensively in warm climates, with bedding on top works well in dry areas. In wettish countries like Britain, the stable intended for such a floor should be sited on the highest part of the yard to ensure that the natural water table is nowhere near the surface! Local authorities in some areas, depending on their attitude to horses in the environment, might not permit such a flooring and might, whatever system is used, try to insist on an expensive drainage system in addition unless expert confirmation could be provided that it is not needed.

I kept a horse for a whole winter on an earth floor under straw bedding. His urine simply drained through the earth, there was no residual wet, the bedding stayed quite dry and there was certainly no smell. I used very much less bedding than I normally would on an ordinary floor, and I always like to have a thick, dry, clean bed whenever horses are in as I feel it is kinder to their legs and it

Fig. 9 This stabling, by Loddon Livestock Equipment Limited, Loddon, Norwich, Norfolk, is ideal for providing accommodation at reasonable cost inside existing buildings or newly-erected American style barns. The horses can see out over the tops of their doors so avoiding the caged-in feeling that often occurs when full, instead of half, doors are used. Between the boxes are bars rather than solid partitions, which again gives more of a feeling of space and allows horses to see the other horses in the building. The attendants have the advantage of working indoors and the aisle in this example is wide enough for a muck-trailer or feed-trolley to be taken down the building, thus facilitating working operations. Depending on the structure of the building, doors could also be provided in the backs of the boxes so the horses could look outside, giving an alternative view, and, indeed, another entrance and exit for safety and convenience.

encourages them to lie down and rest.

Economies on stabling can obviously result in large savings. Brick-built stabling is very expensive for most of us to have erected. Timber is also expensive now – a single timber box can cost anything from just under £500 to £2000, depending on what refinements (such as double skinned walls to the eaves, double insulated roof, overhang, ridge roof ventilators and so on) you choose to have. The object of a stable is of course to protect the horse from the elements and to keep him clean and handy for us. Although 'extras' are desirable, some very adequate boxes of very basic design (little more than four walls and a roof) can be found accommodating healthy, well-kept horses. The main requirements are good ventilation, a view out, shelter from the elements and dry, safe flooring.

If you are having boxes erected, there are any number of suppliers of pre-fabricated boxes (timber) or firms erecting concrete block types. Prices vary tremendously depending on structure and your exact requirements. It is almost always cheaper to convert an existing building if something suitable is available: cattle housing is commonly converted to indoor pony boxes, bull boxes to loose boxes for horses, and so on. The main problem which such conversions is that they often have low ceilings which can be dangerous for horses, although many do live safely in them. Even taking into account the fact that plumbing for waterers and electric fittings often have to be moved or have conduits fitted round them to prevent horses interfering with them, and that floors almost always have to be changed usually for reasons of drainage, conversions are still cheaper than building new.

Premises with old coach houses and stables attached can be restored and the old stalls made into fewer boxes by having front walls put in and extra railings erected between boxes to prevent horses getting at each other. Larger buildings such as barns, if of sound construction, can be made into stabling by the erection of indoor boxes; again, there are several suppliers of excellent internal stabling units advertising in equestrian journals.

There is nothing wrong, of course, with using second-hand materials for economy provided they are strong, and stables do need to be of very strong construction. Corrugated iron and asbestos sheeting, although often seen, are not strong enough and can easily be dismantled by a determined kicker or by a tied-up horse panicking and pulling back until the structure comes down around his ears. This is false economy in the extreme!

It is also bad practice to make stabling out of materials which are good conductors of heat as are metal and asbestos. This makes a stable stiflingly hot in summer and freezing cold in winter. It also encourages a most unhealthy atmosphere inside the stables from which the horse has no escape. Traditional materials are still mainly used for stabling. Brick is certainly the best as it is a good insulator but is expensive. Double layers of wood are good and felts and roofing tiles should have insulating properties or be lined with insulating materials which are, however, not flammable (check with your local Fire Department about suitable materials and also the fire regulations concerning animal housing). Some synthetic stabling materials on the market are both strong and flame-retardant and new ones are coming out all the time.

Much more attention could be paid to ventilation than is normally the case. Simply leaving the top door open is quite inadequate, as is also leaving the window open on the same side of the stable as the door. You need facilities to create overhead cross-draughts by creating louvres or simply a removeable plank or few bricks at eaves height on the wall opposite the door, or, of course, another openable window. Ridge roof ventilators should be standard equipment on all stables in my view so that warm, stale air can rise up and away. The most dangerous pollutants in a stable are those arising from decomposing urine and droppings, particularly ammonia gas which is a heavy gas and gathers in the lower part of the box if there is no draught to remove it. Although floor-level air inlets are often advised in some old and not-so-old books on stable management, I have yet to find a way of providing a floor-level air inlet without also creating a draught. I find the best way to cope is to scatter Stable Boy granules on the swept floor when mucking out (cat litter, bought specially in economy-sized sacks, does just as good a job more cheaply) to absorb the gases to a large extent and also to leave the bottom door open whenever possible such as when the horse is out or in all but bad or very windy weather. You can put a bar, chain or webbing restrainer (an American import available from some saddlers and stable equipment suppliers) to keep the horse in whilst improving his ventilation. Unfortunately, if your horse is the sort who puts his legs everywhere including over the bar, chain or whatever, you cannot do this. In such cases, you might like to fit a cage-type lower inner door.

Anything you can do to improve your horse's stable environment will reduce work and costs in the long run as he will be healthier and need less veterinary attention.

Labour costs can be saved if you or someone in your family is good at doing-it-yourself; otherwise, a competent local handyman can be engaged to convert or erect buildings with strong, used materials.

There can surely be nothing as uneconomical as to go to the trouble and expense of erecting stabling or converting some other building only to be told by your local council to pull it down again because you did not have proper planning permission or did not apply for change of use of the building. Some councils are not only apathetic about providing riding facilities, or even helping with bridleways, but actually antipathetic about having horses in their area at all.

One family in my locality bought a house in a sparsely populated suburb especially because it had an old stable block ripe for renovation and a paddock for their two ponies. The stable block had been used as a garage and general storage place for thirty years but, as it had originally been used for housing horses, they thought nothing of putting it back to its proper use. They spent a good deal of money and effort on the restoration, which was tastefully and properly done, moved the ponies in and promptly received notice from the council to remove them because they did not have permission to keep horses on the premises. They should, apparently, have applied for change of use of the 'garage' back to stabling. They put the ponies at livery, applied for change of use to the building's original purpose and were refused! The house move and renovation had cost them over £5,000.

While on the subject of stabling, it is as well to consider whether in fact you need it at all. A stable is certainly an advantage, particularly if you want to keep a horse in for convenience or if he is sick and needs, indeed probably wishes, to be isolated. But there are other cheaper methods of accommodating horses more appropriate to them.

A method mentioned in chapter 1 is yarding, which I feel could be made much more use of in Britain. Many stable and similar premises do not make the best use of their space. Many a small area could usefully have an open covered run or shed erected and kept bedded on deep litter and the open fenced-in area in front of it floored with some suitable material such as a mixture of peat and sand, woodchips or used bedding minus droppings. A shed for two loose horses, for example, should be a minimum size of 5m (16ft) by 3.5m (12ft). It does not need any special flooring although it is nice to keep it bedded on deep litter as mentioned, the bedding being put straight on to the earth. Such a shed, having no expensive fittings such as windows or doors or a partition to separate the two horses, is considerably cheaper than two stables.

The horses have each other for close company and they have the freedom to be outside in the yard or under cover in the shed as they wish.

The shed – which should, as discussed, be strongly built – can have a long hayrack (as for cattle) down the back wall or rings for haynets. In inclement weather, the horses should be kept in New Zealand rugs because they will spend a good deal of time in the yard out in the open from free choice.

This method, of course, is very similar to keeping horses out in a grass paddock with a field shelter, except that yarded horses do not get anything like as dirty as their paddock-kept counterparts, the flooring material, unlike mud, being easily brushed off.

On the continent of Europe, it is common practice for large herds of breeding stock (not necessarily quiet-natured cold-blooded types of horses but spirited competition breeds and bloodstock) to be out during the day and brought into large, deep-litter barns at night rather than individually stabled. Many stud farms run on such lines would not exist if they had to spend the money and labour involved in stabling their animals in a more conventional way.

Apart from the great savings in time and money, such accommodation arrangements go down very well with the horses, who have a much more natural life associating closely and freely with their own kind. They learn herd manners and are used to being disciplined by their elders and superiors in the herd, and therefore they take to human discipline much more kindly than animals who have been kept in a more unnatural way. These animals are communally fed their concentrates and hay in continuous mangers and hay holders running round the walls of the building.

When it comes to removing droppings, this is of course a chore, but one much more quickly completed than doing the appropriate number of boxes.

The only way to save money on paid labour is, obviously, not to employ it! This of course means that you have to do the work yourself, get a member of your family to do it or take turns with other owners in a communal yard to help each other out. This topic is dealt with in the next chapter.

There are various mechanical means of avoiding the use of paid labour, such as horse-walkers, which are becoming more and more used now, electric groomers, which save a good deal of time, heat

lamps in boxes to dry off wet horses or simple means such as riding
one horse and leading another and so exercising two horses (or
even three if you have one on each side, your horses are very well
behaved and your area has very few, and very considerate, road
users) in the time it normally takes to do only one. Turning
animals out saves some exercising but doesn't maintain fitness.

The first three methods obviously involve the expenditure of
money on buying the equipment, but they save money on paid
labour in the long run. If paid labour is out of the question
anyway, they save work for you or enable you to do more horses
and to get jobs done more quickly than you otherwise would. Time
saving and money saving are very closely linked in many areas.

Feeding, stabling and labour are significantly expensive items in
horse management. Another expensive item, and one which often
comes as a shock to new horse owners, is shoeing. A horse doing
two hours' work a day, much of it on roads, will surely wear out a
set of shoes in six weeks, and maybe sooner if the roads used have
a chippings surface rather than a smooth tarmac one.

It is often thought that using heavier shoes will give longer wear,
but in fact this is not so. Using heavy rather than medium-weight
shoes simply causes the feet to be brought down on the road
harder, creating more wear, in fact, on the shoe and more
concussion on the foot and leg. Medium-weight shoes are the
choice of most people for riding and lightweight driving horses
doing road work, and such horses can cope with that weight easily
without having their action affected.

Reducing wear on the shoes enables them to be removed when
the feet need trimming and then replaced. Apart from using soft
surfaces such as tracks and verges whenever possible, another
method of reducing wear is to get your farrier to weld into the toes
and heels, or any areas which the horse wears unevenly, some
hardener such as boron. Whatever the farrier uses, just make sure
it is a hardener which wears rough, not smooth, to help prevent
slipping.

Many horses and ponies are shod which do not actually need to be,
creating unnecessary expense. If your horse's work is mainly on
soft surfaces or, for limited distances, hard, smooth roads, and if
his foot conformation and quality of horn are good and he is on a
balanced diet which will help maintain the horn quality, there is no
reason why he should not go barefoot. This suggestion is discussed
further in chapter 7 but, for information, it is not unlawful for

you to *trim* your horse's feet yourself even if you are not a qualified, registered farrier. The unlawful part comes when you try to nail shoes on to the feet. There is no law which stops you obtaining training to enable you to do this job, if you can find someone to show you how to do it. Even if you cannot, provided you understand how the foot should be balanced – and provided your horse does not have any exaggerated faulty action which would create grossly uneven wear – learning to trim and maintain your horse's feet is not *that* difficult.

If you cannot find a farrier who will show you how, study of a good book on farriery (such as *Farriery* by John Hickman (Allen)) plus common sense and practice will enable you to do a competent job. I know of several people who are having to work along these lines from force of circumstance, being unable to obtain the services of a good farrier in their area.

Transporting your horse to events of various kinds can be a considerable expense. If you are doing a lot of travelling, it is obviously very much more convenient to have your own transport than to have to rely on others, and much cheaper than having constant transporter's bills to pay. Obviously, a horsebox needs road tax, but you could tax it only during the seasons you are using it. It is also another vehicle which needs maintaining, but it does score over a trailer in comfort, ride and safety.

As we are specifically considering economies in this chapter, it has to be said that a trailer costs less to buy than a box carrying the same number of horses – unless, possibly, you compare a *de luxe* new trailer with a sound but aged horsebox. There is no road tax for a trailer, but it will doubtless cost more on your car insurance. Your car's transmission in particular will undergo more wear, and you might need to purchase a larger, more powerful car, particularly if you are going to transport two or more horses in the trailer.

Clubbing together with friends for contracted transport is, of course, fairly economical, although if not enough of you wish to go to a particular event to fill the only box the contractor has available it could prove more expensive than you had bargained for. Do not, in pursuit of excessive economy, be tempted to put up with a vehicle which is unsafe, either as regards roadworthiness or as regards the comfort and safety of the animals travelling in it. Cattle waggons are often used for horses by contract transport firms; these do not have proper partitions, simply bars between animals who often have to travel sideways in very cramped conditions. They can easily fall and there is nothing to stop them from being trodden on and seriously injured by their neighbours.

If you 'hitch a lift' to an event in a friend's transport, be sure there is no question of 'hire and reward', i.e. that you do not pay him or her for taking you or you could find that whatever insurance cover your friend has is negated. (A contribution towards petrol, however, is another matter.) This whole business of insurance regarding 'amateur' horse transportation is a very grey area and, as you will doubtless want some compensation from somebody if your horse is injured during transportation, you would be well advised to check on your own insurance and check with your friend before taking the plunge.

It has to be said that if an insurance company can avoid paying out on a claim, then it will surely do so. Insurance companies are in business to make money and will hang on to it like any successful business if they possibly can. Make quite sure you fully understand the terms of your policy. This is no easy matter, even with a basic policy, so do not hesitate to get confirmation from the company *in writing* of any point creating uncertainty. Discuss the matter with a solicitor if you feel you are being 'fobbed off' by the company on any point not answered clearly, or if they refuse to put an explanation in black and white.

Insuring your horse is another dicey business sometimes. Again, there are many, many complaints about insurance companies finding ways of not paying out on claims – particularly for loss of use, when it seems that their vet invariably disagrees with yours! There have been cases reported in the press where a horse was kept suffering unnecessarily because the insurance company insisted on a vet of its choice travelling to see the animal and refusing to take the policy-holder's vet's opinion as satisfactory in cases where slaughter was recommended. Conversely, animals have been put down due to accident or sudden severe illness without the policy-holder's being able to contact the insurance company (say, at a weekend) to advise them of the situation, and these policy-holders have later been denied their payout because of this. I and several people I know have suffered at the hands of insurance companies and, because of our experiences, now feel that the only insurances worth having are third-party insurance (which you get free if you are a member of the British Horse Society) and insurance to cover veterinary fees.

Some companies reduce premiums if horses are kept on shredded paper bedding and/or fed hay-age because of the reduced risk of respiratory disorders.

Even with veterinary fees cover, however, there can be points to watch with some companies. If you claim for, say, a sprained tendon, you could find that the company exclude all future cover for disorders in that leg. If the horse once has a cough and you claim for veterinary attention, you may never again get cover for a respiratory disorder of any kind. Even if you *can* get cover, the premium could be raised considerably because you have claimed in the past.

So, the only advice I can give on insurance – which is backed up by experience – is that cover for death or loss of use of your horse is so expensive and so uncertain that it is not worth the expenditure. Cover for veterinary fees is well worthwhile, but before you sign check up on what will happen to future claims regarding related disorders and get a satisfactory explanation in writing. Third-party insurance is essential, but it is cheaper for you to join the British Horse Society (The British Equestrian Centre, Stoneleigh, Kenilworth, Warwickshire, CV8 2LR), whose membership fee is cheaper than the premium you would have to pay. And you not only get many additional benefits in cash and kind from being a B.H.S. member – you are also helping the wide-ranging cause of equestrianism and horse and pony welfare by joining. You may personally feel it worthwhile asking about the pros and cons of insuring your tack against theft or damage, your horse against theft and also looking into personal accident insurance in connection with your riding activities. There are various offers available from the many insurance companies involved in this field and I feel the best plan is to get a few personal recommendations from friends, colleagues and other contacts, particularly asking about particular companies' records on actually paying out and whether there was a great deal of unreasonable hassle involved in the process. Most companies will give a significant discount for security-marked tack or a freeze-marked horse. Indeed, as regards the latter, many people feel it is not worthwhile insuring a marked horse as statistics show that the chances of the horse being stolen (as against an unmarked horse) and not recovered are very slim, but this is a matter for personal choice.

Cash-saving Tips

- Feed hay in the field in such a way that it cannot be trampled in the mud or blown away. Feed concentrates in tip-proof containers or hold the bucket of a messy feeder to prevent waste.
- It's cheaper to keep your horse at a 'commune'-type stable where you take it in turns to do the chores and help each other out, than to pay livery/labour fees because you haven't time to make two or more trips daily to the yard.
- Always buy in bulk when you can, maybe with friends, as it is cheaper than buying in smaller quantities.
- Be mean with the yard electricity. Although lights are a good security measure, and horses do not like pitch darkness, keep levels very low if you are leaving them on all night. Sensor-operated security lights are very bright but only come on when the beam is activated.
- Try making your own haynets out of binder twine.
- Run a horsey car-boot sale or flea market for the surrounding horse owners. As well as getting cash for your unwanted bits and pieces, you could buy some bargains from other sellers.
- Buy the best quality you can afford of everything as it will last much longer.
- But don't pay through the nose for imported horse feeds. This is truly false economy perpetrated by old-fashioned professionals (particularly, I find, in the racing world) who do not understand modern feeding science and don't realise that the modern branded feeds are cheaper and more effective, not to mention more reliable, than an unproven mixture of unknown composition which costs the earth.
- A thick bed is more economical than a thin one and does its job better.
- Don't begrudge the cost of identity-coding your horse. It's cheaper and less painful than replacing him.
- Effective worm control is one of the most effective methods of saving money on feed, even taking into account the cost of the wormers.
- Do keep your feeds in damp- and vermin-proof containers to avoid waste and contamination. Do use an old fridge for storing perishable feeds such as molassed feeds, soaked/soaking sugar beet pulp and so on.
- Keep your insurance premiums up to date so that previous ones

are not wasted should you make a claim two days after yours has
run out!

- Keep vaccinations up to date, too, as you'll have the expense of
having to re-do the whole programme if you are a day 'out'
when it comes to competing.
- If feeding extra oil or fat to your horse, use corn, maize or soya
oil as it's cheaper than cod liver oil specifically marketed for
horses.
- For short periods in the field, diluted TCP makes a cheap fly
repellant.
- Disposable nappies are good for retaining heat on legs or feet
when poulticing.
- Make feed measures by cutting the bottom off lemonade bottles
and so on and stick on a label stating how much, by weight, of
each food it holds.
- Apart from being a natural antiseptic, garlic in the feed, or
diluted and boiled, makes a fair insect repellant.
- Baby oil is cheaper than branded show-coat conditioners, but
don't overdo it.
- Get together with other owners and try to have the farrier and
vet's visits (for example, for annual health/vaccination procedures) on the same day to save on visit fees.
- Get your farrier to weld hardening materials into the most-worn
parts of your horse's shoes, for extra wear.
- Borrow items from friends if you only need them occasionally,
rather than buying – but be sure to return them and also return
the favour when asked!
- Learn to do basic tack and clothing repairs and adaptations
yourself rather than buying new all the time. When buying
second-hand clothing to save cash, always disinfect it before use
and preferably buy from a source where you know the horse has
been healthy.
- It's cheaper to get a saddler to adapt items of tack than to buy
new, such as making a running martingale into a standing one or
adapting a cavesson noseband to become a flash. You can make
a useful bitless bridle out of a sturdy, strengthened drop
noseband and a pair of reins.
- Buy good quality, guaranteed second-hand tack from a reputable saddler rather than new, and have it altered to fit your horse,
if appropriate.
- Think before you buy anything! You should be asking yourself

what you can manage without rather than what you can do with!

- Save binder twine and the thread from the tops of feed sacks. They come in useful for all sorts of things from making haynets, running emergency repairs to rugs, fencing, fillet strings, halters and head-collars and so on.
- Don't spend money on expensive items that sound good in adverts unless you are certain you need them – this goes for everything from feed supplements to saddles.
- Weigh out feeds accurately so you feed correctly. Feeding too much is expensive, wasteful and can harm your horse.
- Don't buy more perishable feed (like coarse mixes, molassine meal or even straight grains) than you can use within a safe period (depending on the product) as it will go 'off' and will be wasted.
- Grow your own hydroponic grass at home using old roasting tins or plastic ice-cream containers on open bookshelves in a window. Even home units can cost hundreds of pounds!
- Don't keep hay where it is exposed to the weather as this ruins it and leaches out nutrients, creating waste.
- Experiments have shown that soaking hay for over-long periods also removes most of the nutrients. Eight hours should be enough.
- Well-cared-for grass is far cheaper than bought-in feed.
- Blankets can be bought in domestic-store sales or charity shops and are cheaper than 'proper' horse blankets. Never mind the colour!
- Do you really need a proper grooming tidy? Use a water bucket instead.
- Buy second-hand wood for fence repairs and jumps.
- House-train your horse! By training your horse to associate, say, a particular low whistling sound with staling you can get him to stale more or less on command outside the stable or into a bucket with a little bedding in the bottom (to avoid the noise and splash which horses hate) and so save on bedding. Get him to stale outside or into the bucket when you return from a ride – and remember, many horses stale when you put down a new bed, so be ready with the bucket!

4 A little help from your friends

Anyone who undertakes the care of a horse takes on a considerable responsibility not only for his conduct but for his welfare too, directly and indirectly. People mistreating animals, whether their own or other people's, can, under the law, be prosecuted, fined and banned from keeping them for specified periods.

Horse owners who delegate the care of their horse to another person, or people, are still responsible for the animal's welfare. It is up to them to supervise and see that those other people are, in fact, properly carrying out their duties in relation to the horse's care. Horse owners who look after their horses single-handedly obviously have total responsibility; even if they fall ill, the horse still has to be cared for and in such circumstances it is up to them to obtain other help to see to the horse.

This often raises a big problem for those keeping horses either at home or in other accommodation with no other help at all. Not only are they tied as regards their daily routine, but life can become very difficult if they are ill or injured to the extent that they are seriously incapacitated, even for a short time. There is a great deal to be said for independence, but just as much for being part of a group, even a small one, of like-minded people who work together to help each other out, either just during emergencies or as a matter of course.

If you do want to keep your horse at home – for many people having their horse outside the back door, as it were, is the only way they will be really happy about keeping a horse at all – and there is no other member of the family competent to help or in any way involved with your horsy activities, why not consider providing free stabling, grazing and part-time care to one or two other animals in return for companionship for your horse and help from their owners, either on a regular basis or at times specified by you? These owners would be responsible for all their own costs regarding feed, bedding, shoeing, veterinary expenses, etc. but would simply not pay for their stabling and grazing or for the occasional labour you put into their horses. In turn, it would be understood that they agree to help with your horse or horses according to a mutually acceptable agreement.

Such an arrangement can work extremely well for all parties concerned provided you all get on together. Livery stable proprietors are well used to being nice to people they don't particularly like! They are in business for money and although they may prefer to work on a friendly basis with their clients it is not essential to them. Of course, any owners who are a real pain in the neck or are totally unreasonable in their demands or behaviour can be told to take their unwelcome patronage elsewhere.

When you are considering having other people and horses on your own private premises, not for business but to establish what it is hoped will be a mutually beneficial, friendly working relationship, you naturally do not want people around whose ideas of horsmastership differ drastically from your own, whom you do not like or trust or who you simply can't talk to. 'Interviewing' a horse and owner for such a scheme, then, is rather like choosing a friend and an employee in one.

Not only do you have to like both horses and owners reasonably well. You must also get straight between you exactly how the horses are going to be cared for: if the owners' principles differ greatly from yours, you will not be happy having to treat their horses in a manner with which you disagree, and you are also going to be worried that they will not carry out your wishes and systems in your absence, no matter what assurances they give. A straightforward, honest discussion should, therefore, take place before any promises are made. Everything should be clear – what amount of work they will be expected to do in exchange for their free stabling, grazing and part-time care (the provision of which could save them anywhere in the region of £30 a week at current rates), who will be responsible for the maintenance of the stable and where you draw the line between reasonable wear and tear and wilful damage on the part of their horses. It should also be stressed that their horses will have to be wormed at the same time and with the same product (drug) as yours for the sake of keeping your pasture 'clean'. It only takes one infested horse to infect a paddock and give the other horses on it a continuous worm burden, no matter how carefully they themselves are wormed, so everyone must be in agreement on this important point. Similarly with vaccinations: it is pointless some horses being protected from influenza if one horse is not, falls victim to every epidemic going and brings the virus home. Vaccinations give a *level* of protection. If infection is at a high level in the yard because one particular horse has a bad case of 'flu, the vaccinated horses might also succumb to a mild case of it.

Having straightened out everything of this nature and found, either through the grapevine or from advertising locally, people and horses you feel you can work with and get on with reasonably well (and vice versa), you may well find that you actually prefer having someone else around to ease your workload a bit and to socialise with, particularly if you are a sociable type of person. Such arrangements can work very well for all concerned if gone into sensibly.

Do-It-Yourself Livery Accommodation

This type of livery is becoming more and more popular with owners as a means of keeping costs down. Like any other system, it has advantages and disadvantages. The best way is to use a yard with an official manager who will oversee owners without being felt to interfere. Owners can still do their horses according to their own principles, but any cases of actual neglect or mistreatment can be dealt with. The person concerned will, if inexperienced, have matters explained so that he or she knows better in future, while those who refuse to improve will be 'sacked', perhaps with a simultaneous report to an animal welfare organisation, too, in bad enough cases.

Such yards are often found as part of a riding school or livery centre proper. Particularly in areas where full liveries are hard to obtain, or where a riding school does not want to be particularly bothered with normal liveries, they can provide good revenue for the yard proprietor. Liveries of any kind bring in regular income all year round and make up for the sometimes erratic income provided by the riding school part of the business, which may be prone to seasonal fluctuations particularly if it has no indoor school.

Other types of do-it-yourself livery accommodation may be found in various premises which are simply available for rent with no formal supervision of any kind, such as former riding schools or other horse businesses which have closed down, old farm buildings, private premises whose owners simply wish to get a little (or sometimes significant) extra income without having any work involved. Such yards can create problems with less-than-responsible owners neglecting their animals. Unlike a managed yard, where the reputation of the entire establishment will matter to the manager, unsupervised yards have no one who cares about this sort of thing. The other owners will have no one to report problems to and may be looking after their own horses in an unpleasant, slapdash atmosphere with which they will not be happy.

A major problem arises in any kind of rented accommodation or livery arrangement where the premises have no living accommodation and so have no one there overnight or even, sometimes, during the day. This leaves the horses wide open to theft and abuse, and it is a very poor way indeed to keep a horse. To leave horses alone and not checked on for many hours, or even to leave them out of earshot should any horse start thrashing about with colic or some other painful disorder, is extremely poor horsemastership. I personally feel it would be better not to own a horse at all than to keep one under such circumstances, as it is simply grossly unfair to the animal.

A Mutual Co-operation Society

The advantages of having help available have been discussed and I feel there is everything to be gained by all the owners in a do-it-yourself livery establishment, managed or not, getting together and working out ways in which they can all help each other – not only in emergencies but on a regular daily basis to ease each other's burdens.

Why not call an informal meeting, either in the yard or at someone's house and put forward your ideas of how you could all help each other? If your yard has a manager she (it usually is a 'she') should certainly be invited, as she will be the linchpin of the operation, not actually being roped in with the work except in genuine emergency but seeing that messages reach the right people and that each horse is properly cared for.

In the north of England there is a saying that 'there's nowt so queer as folk', and it's very true. To make any 'commune' type of

arrangement work, you all have to be reasonable people –
individuals, obviously, with your own ideas of horse management
and of varying standards, but able to work with your colleagues
together for one main aim: to ensure that all the horses and ponies
on the yard are looked after while, at the same time, saving each
other money by the methods detailed in chapter 3 and, particularly,
saving each other time by helping out. You really need a yardful of
sensible, mature people to make things work. However, children
often keep their ponies under such arrangements and this can be
valuable training for them, character forming and instilling a sense
of responsibility.

Any horse needs attending to at least twice in twenty-four hours.
This involves two trips, two lots of petrol or fares, two lots of
commuting time and two lots of chores for each owner to perform,
but if friends/associates get together and agree (even just two
friends working together) that one does the horses in the morning
and the other at night, think how much easier your day will be.

Imagine a do-it-yourself yard – purely imaginary, I stress –
comprising the following people, with their differing time availability and hours of work.

There is a young secretary whose job is largely nine to five but
who works 'flexitime' on occasion; a hospital doctor who works
long but erratic hours and who is often at the yard at 'peculiar'
times; a factory worker who works irregular shifts on a regular
basis (i.e. three day shifts, then three afternoon shifts and finally
three night shifts, followed by three or four days off); a shop
worker who works mainly nine to five-thirty but all day most
Saturdays, with two half-days off (not always the same two) during
the week; a vicar who never calls on Sundays but often attends
during the day on Saturdays and in the week; two teenagers who
are at a nearby school and attend to their ponies morning and late
afternoon, Monday to Friday, and, of course, nearly all weekend;
and finally a freelance instructress who keeps her horse at the yard
and attends when not out on teaching appointments.

The yard also has a manager, who takes messages and generally
oversees operations to make sure every animal is properly looked
after.

A rota has been drawn up, by mutual discussion and agreement,
in this yard and is written on a blackboard in the tack room. Those
with irregular working hours advise in advance when they will be
available. In every case, when one owner's allocated jobs cannot

be fulfilled because of his or her absence, someone else takes over.

The secretary's wage is quite low, but instead of paying rent she helps the yard proprietor with correspondence on a regular basis. She can arrive at her job at 10 a.m. on certain days provided that she makes the time up at some point by staying until 6 p.m. She usually does this, as the two teenagers come to the yard straight from school and can be there to see to her horse at 4.30 p.m., in exchange for her having fed theirs and turned them out in the morning.

The shop assistant and the instructress are both present early each day and see to the animals whose owners are not coming that morning, feeding and turning out those required according to their owners' instructions for the day as noted in the 'master diary' in the tack room (see chapter 6).

On her afternoons off, the shop assistant often exercises someone else's horse as well as her own, in exchange for them exercising hers on a Saturday when she cannot normally come. The instructress, for her part, is sometimes away for several days taking a course, but repays the others for looking after her horse during these times by giving them free class lessons and help with schooling problems.

The yard manager keeps the blackboard and master diary up to date by writing in owners' telephone messages and, on the rare occasions when no one at all can be in the yard at a certain time, will feed, skip out, water and bring horses in and out from the field. If her duties become significant, the owners pay for them separately from their rent out of their kitty budget.

I once kept a horse in a do-it-yourself livery yard without an official manager. The yard was owned by an elderly but fairly active lady who would always help by throwing hay over doors and filling buckets from a hosepipe. Our kitty budget regularly paid for the services of a freelance groom at times when none of us could get to the yard and the system worked very well, particularly as the owner lived on the premises and we had two shift workers among us who could usually be present when those working regular hours could not.

As you can see, then, a group of people *can* work together to ensure that, while they still have time to enjoy their own horses, *all* the animals in the yard are looked after at least adequately by means of mutual co-operation, a flexible rota, fair play and organisation. They all know each other's animals and their foibles

well and take an interest in them, so they gain a wider experience of
horses and horsemastership than would be the case if they restricted
their activities to just one animal, their own.

If you keep your horse at home and do not want, or haven't
room for, other people's horses on the premises, you may well be
able to rope in at least one member of your family to help while
you are at work or away from home, or obtain the occasional
services of a freelance groom. Agencies, which usually advertise in
equestrian journals, have a pool of temporary/occasional help on
which you can draw, so keep the telephone numbers of at least two
handy.

You're On Your Own!

If you really are on your own, you will simply have to manage by
means of super-organised efficiency and willpower. If your whole
family is going on holiday together, send the horse away to livery
rather than keeping him at home with no one there, in the hands
of a temporary groom who only comes in morning and evening.
You might get away with leaving him at home if you have a very
close neighbour who will help, but personally I should not want to
leave a horse of mine for long periods unsupervised.

Feed Charts

Probably the single aspect of management most likely to cause
problems when horses are being looked after by people other than
their owners is feeding. Even though you know your horse's diet
inside out, it is essential, where others are involved, to leave clear
and precise details of what he should have for each feed, either in
a book, on a chart pinned on the wall, or on a communal
blackboard used for everyone in a yard. Put exact details in weight
rather than simply saying 'a scoop of coarse mix' or 'a spoon of
supplement', for reasons of both general health and economy.
Horses have very delicate digestive systems and will not tolerate
too many irregularities in feeding, so write it all down.

5 Time for everything

We all have the same amount of time – twenty-four hours in each day–night cycle – yet how often do we hear the complaint: 'I haven't got *time* to do that.' Of course, those who say that mean they have too much else to do, but I wonder if they have ever thought seriously not only about how much they commit themselves to but how they do the things they do anyway.

If you constantly feel pressured, if you find it hard to concentrate on what you are doing at this minute and are constantly thinking about what you have to do next, tomorrow, next week or next month, if you get bad tempered easily, even with those you love, if you frequently feel tired, not just healthily, physically tired but draggingly weary, and if you find that you do not seem to get much real *enjoyment* out of life, not even out of your horse whom you are supposedly keeping for fun – the chances are you are either genuinely doing too much or are not doing what you do do efficiently.

The subject of 'time management' has become big business in the business world. Large and small companies spend many hundreds, even thousands, of pounds each year sending their key managers on expensive but usually worthwhile time management courses. There are umpteen good books on time management, all giving a slightly different view of the subject but all agreeing on one main key principle: to manage your time effectively you have to get your priorities right. Setting and judging priorities is the most valuable lesson you can learn, from either a course or a book. You must evaluate your tasks accurately so that you are sure which are the most *important* (not necessarily which are the most *urgent*, because you'll have to do those anyway). Then write them down as if you were giving someone a list of things to do.

You may think: 'What's the point of that? I don't need to write things down. I *know* what I've got to do – too much!' You will find, however, that if you make a habit of writing yourself what is

commonly called a 'To-Do List' it will crystallise everything
wonderfully for you; it will act as a constant 'conscience' and you
will get a super feeling of smugness and self-satisfaction when you
look at your list of tasks at the end of the day, all crossed off with
everything done. There is no need to write every little detail on the
list, but you will find it beneficial to extend it to all areas of your
life – horse, home, work/business, social – as this gives you a clear
picture of the whole of your life's activities and you can see if any
one aspect is taking a disproportionate precedence over the others.

Many time managers recommend that you keep a time log for a
week so that you can see what you *really* spend most of your time
doing. It is easy to think you are spending more time on one task
than you really are. It is just as easy to overlook just how much
time is really taken up in reading the newspaper or sitting looking
at your in-tray; out of the window wondering if anyone has brought
your horse in; at the basket of ironing that you have to do; at the
pile of correspondence you never seem to catch up with. In fact,
wondering how on earth you are ever going to get everything done
is just about the worst way to spend your time, because during that
time you are doing precisely nothing – and that is a complete waste
of time. It's not even an enjoyable nothing like dreaming what
you'd do if you won half a million pounds on the pools. It is an
aggravating, depressing kind of nothing.

So stop wondering how you are going to get everything done.
There is only one way to get *anything* done – and that is to get on
with it!

Fortunately for horse owners, a vital key to time management –
setting priorities – is easy, at least as regards the horse-orientated
tasks. You simply put the horse first. Make a list of absolutely
every single job, big or small, you have to do in relation to your
horse, and then divide them into 'A' jobs and 'B' jobs. The 'A'
jobs are those which directly affect your horse and the 'B' jobs are
those which are connected with his care but which do not directly
affect his welfare.

Put yourself in your horse's position to help you prioritise the
jobs you have listed. Just imagine what *he* would care about. He
would care about getting his food and water, he would care about
getting out of his box and stretching his legs, he would care about
having somewhere away from his own excreta to stand and lie,
about his rugs being made comfortable and about having clean
water to drink. On the other hand, he wouldn't care at all about

straw blowing about the yard, about paintwork peeling, about the untidy tack room or about the sprawling muck heap.

The following is a short list of what I consider to be 'A' jobs, those which should take priority during your 'horse time' and which are all very important because they directly affect the horse:

- Feeding/watering
- Mucking out/skipping out
- Adjusting/changing rugs
- Cleaning feed and water containers
- Maintaining stable (so it does not fall down on top of him)
- Exercising
- Picking out feet, cleaning eyes, nose and dock
- Cleaning underside of tack (which touches horse)
- Maintaining fencing (so horse can be turned out)

Now here is a list of (in my book) 'B' jobs which, although important, do not directly affect the horse himself and so should not take priority over 'A' jobs:

- Full grooming (in between 'A' and 'B'!)
- Sweeping yard
- Stacking feed/hay/bedding
- Painting woodwork
- Full tack-cleaning
- Tidying tack room
- Cleaning tools
- Tending muck heap

If some readers are horror-struck at my list, I should stress that this book is intended for people who are keeping horses on a very limited time budget. Anyone with a job to do, a business to run or a young family to look after has limited time. It is quite possible for one horse to take up a whole working day if we let him. Work really does expand to fill the time available for its completion (I can't remember who said that but it's very true) but I prefer to turn things around and make the work diminish so that I spend more of my valuable time doing the things I really want to do, like riding my horse or just being with him, rather than sweeping the yard or cleaning tack, rooting out drawers or cleaning the windows.

I have a particular aversion to spending my time looking after a muck heap. I cringe every time I hear some well-meaning expert say 'a tidy muck heap is a sign of a tidy mind'. Even in the case of a busy riding school or other professional yard but particularly in the case of a working horse owner, a tidy muck heap is a sign of someone who hasn't got his or her priorities right. The state of your horse is far more important than the state of your muck heap.

If all your 'A' jobs are done, and your horse is either contentedly munching hay in his box, having had enjoyable, slightly taxing exercise, or is in the field enjoying the company of his friends (something you both enjoy), then it is time to get stuck into all those 'B' jobs – now that you've nothing more important to do!

You can make things even clearer for yourself by prioritising jobs within categories, e.g. numbering jobs, A1, A2, A3 and so on, and the same with the Bs – not to put them in order of carrying them out, which you should automatically know (exercising always comes before feeding, for example), but in order of importance. The idea is simply to make sure you don't waste valuable horse time, or daylight hours in winter, sweeping the yard, for instance, when the horse needs exercising. Get the horse out first, feed him, make him comfortable for the night, and sweep the yard (if you must) by electric light or by the light of your car headlights, as I've done many a time. (That teaches you to be quick, too, especially if your car battery is on its last legs!)

In fact, working more quickly, without rushing and skimping things, is a definite asset. Imagine that it normally takes you half an hour to groom your horse and half an hour to muck out his box. Give yourself, instead, twenty-five minutes to do each task and work just that bit more quickly. You will then save ten minutes, which you can use to scrub out his feed and water containers, or stay out ten minutes longer at exercise, or run over the underside of your bridle, a job which otherwise might not have got done.

Now imagine that you have only half an hour to spare before you have to, say, pick up your daughter from Brownies. There are two jobs which need doing: your horse needs grooming and the yard needs sweeping. Which are you going to do? You are going to groom the horse, of course! Alternatively, as that was rather a simple choice (the yard being a definite 'B' job) imagine the horse needs grooming *and* mucking out, both half-hour jobs, so you only have time for one of them. Why not sponge your horse's eyes, nostrils, sheath or teats and dock, dandy off the worst stable stains

Figs 10 and 11 Horsewalkers are now an accepted way of giving horses in a busy yard some of their daily exercise. This model, by Equitus of Burnt Ash House, Cirencester Road, Chalford, Stroud, Gloucestershire, does not take up space for its own special area. Its arms fold up out of the way when out of use so it can be erected in an existing schooling area, as shown. This model is available for one to six horses.

and mud, pick out feet into the muck skip then skip out the droppings and very worst of the bedding, scrape in some clean from the sides and then put some fresh bedding on top and banked up round the sides? That way you have ensured your horse's immediate comfort and been in time to pick up your daughter.

Without wishing to try to tell you how to run your private life, this system can also be extended to your domestic chores. If it is your job to prepare the family's evening meal and to wash the car, which is the most important? The meal, of course. The car might get away with just the windows being cleaned for safety's sake.

Once you have determined job priorities, you can make out a timetable showing what you should be doing when. This might sound regimented and unnecessary, but in practice it can give wonderful peace of mind to know that you are running to schedule. Because you are doing what you should be doing when you should be doing it, you automatically know that by keeping to the timetable everything *will* get done in its own good time – provided, of course, that no Act of God occurs to prevent it. While you are out exercising, you don't need to worry about getting the tack cleaned because you know that you have allocated a slot for it at home in the evening, perhaps while you are watching the news on T.V.

I do know people who take listmaking and timetabling too far and who live their entire lives by the clock. It is much better to relate it just to things other than your free time. I suppose by scheduling yourself some free time, say between eight and eleven, you are in fact scheduling that, too – but at least you needn't put: '8 p.m. to 9 p.m. read book, 9 p.m. to 9.30 p.m. write thank-you letters for birthday presents, 9.30 p.m. to 10.30 p.m. . . .' and so on!

If you try the timetable system for a while, just to see how it suits you, you could well find that it really does help to keep you on course; ultimately it will become second nature to you and you can discard the timetable, just making out a new one if circumstances change. I still recommend a written job list, however, particularly for jobs which don't automatically need doing every day – then you can be sure you never forget anything which it is easy for a busy mind to do.

If you leave it long enough, there could come a time when a 'B' job becomes an 'A' job. For instance, not sweeping the yard could result in a yard so strewn with litter that it is actually dangerous.

Fig. 12 Hanging or travelling mangers like these are very good for providing feeds quickly to outdoor horses without having to actually go into the field and possibly fight your way through a milling herd. They can simply be slotted on to a fence rail like this. It is advisable to feed the horse at the top of the pecking order first (if you don't he will just barge in anyway) and so on down the line. There should be at least one more manger of feed available than there are horses to be fed. If there is time, it is far preferable for someone to stay and see fair play for the lower-ranking animals. Any animal not getting his fair ration with this system should be brought out of the field and fed separately. These mangers prevent feed being tipped out into the mud, as can happen with boisterous animals fed with simple bowls or buckets, but do not prevent its being scooped up over the side.

Note that this fencing is only two-rail post and rail. This is quite adequate for mature animals and much cheaper than the normal three- or four-rail type. The rails are inside the posts, presenting a smooth barrier, and the top rail is flush with the tops of the posts, so there is no projection to injure a horse should it try to jump out.

Then it has become an 'A' and should be scheduled accordingly. It is all a matter of common sense and individual circumstance and decision.

Saving time on individual tasks is also a matter for individual preference and circumstance. The only ways to save time on exercising are to turn the horse out for some of his exercise, to use a horse-walker if you have one available or to ride-and-lead. More and more professional and 'full-time amateur' yards now have horse-walkers and find them a boon. Some insist that they could not run their operations without them. They take from one to eight horses, and they normally have walk and trot speeds. If space for the machine is a problem, there is on the market now a model with arms which fold up out of the way so that the walker can be sited in an ordinary schooling area without being a nuisance.

The most time-saving method of bedding is certainly deep litter. You can skip out and replenish bedding in a dozen boxes on deep litter in the time it takes you to fully muck out one. Semi-deep litter, where droppings and the worst of the bedding are removed, cleanish bedding brought in from the sides of the box and a layer of fresh material put on top, works well for many working owners, on a permanent basis or just during the week with full mucking-out taking place only at weekends.

It takes a fit, experienced groom half an hour to thoroughly groom a horse, and more if the horse is going to be wisped as well. For those not so experienced or fit (grooming *is* quite hard work) it takes longer. Working owners simply might not have the time to groom fully every day, and in this connection it has to be said that the horse will not die if you miss a day – or even two – provided essentials like sponging discharges from eyes, nostrils, sheath/teats and dock are attended to and, vitally important, the feet are picked out and shoes (if worn) checked twice daily.

It is true that the grooming process is, if you do it considerately, enjoyable to most horses. It stimulates the skin, gives them close contact with you and builds up a bond of trust and respect between horse and owner. I am certainly not advocating that it should be neglected as a regular thing, simply that if you are really pushed for time then a lick and a promise is quite acceptable. Quartering the horse before you exercise makes him presentable, of course. The essential point to remember is to make sure saddle patch and head are free of mud and dried sweat, otherwise tack or harness put on top of them could rub the horse sore and maybe even develop galls, not only causing pain and discomfort but making exercise difficult until the galls have healed.

If you make a habit of shampooing your horse occasionally, say once a week, weather permitting, this will keep him cleaner longer and you will not need to spend so long manually grooming him on other days. Grooming machines, too, have been around for a long time. The most efficient are the type with a rotary brush and a vacuum facility. The rotary brush takes the elbow grease out of the job for you and the vacuum prevents you from being covered in dust and dandruff. These machines also help accustom horses to

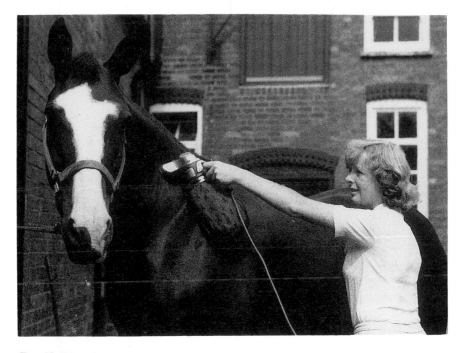

Fig. 13 Electric groomers certainly save time and energy in grooming. This handy model, by Equequip of 7 Pepper Alley, Banbury, Oxfordshire, combines rotary brushes with a vacuum facility and a bag to take the dirt.

being clipped as they exert a slight 'pull' on the skin and make a noise from the motor, both of which clipping machines also do. With either machine, if your horse plays up then stuff cotton wool in his ears and/or play the radio (or sing to him!) to disguise the noise. If you are tactful he will soon get used to it.

Grooming machines can be expensive and you may well consider the expenditure ridiculous, particularly when the suggestion appears in a book devoted to saving money as well as time in horse care. However, as pointed out earlier, it is sometimes necessary to spend one in order to save the other. Spending money on a grooming machine will certainly save you time in grooming your horse and most people who have good machines (the combined rotary brush/vacuum models) would not be without them. They also save a lot of energy, something you are also likely to be short of it you are a working owner.

Another aid to grooming which costs money but saves time is an infra-red lamp in the horse's box or, in a big yard, in a special drying-off box. Shampooing has already been recommended as saving time. In bad weather, particularly if the horse has been out in the rain and the mud (whether ridden or just in the field), these lamps are a real boon. Simply rinse off mud, scrape off excess moisture, dry heels and backs of pasterns with an old, rough towel and leave the horse standing under the lamp while he eats his feed or hay. No rugs or thatching are needed. Even in his winter coat, he will be warm and dry in an hour, ready to be rugged up. They are relaxing for the horse, too, and seem to significantly help prevent breaking out. There are various models on the market averaging about £20 to buy and a very few pence an hour to run. Again, people who have them regard them as a real asset.

An item of equipment which facilitates mucking out is a really good, big barrow, and here the type with an axle and two wheels is ideal for a fairly small yard. The capacity means that you probably only need one trip to the muck heap per box on full mucking out, which saves time and work. However, a single-wheeled barrow holding that much muck would be quite difficult to balance, steer and push, manure being so heavy – it is not that difficult for the barrow to tip and spill some, if not all, of its load on to the yard, making another unnecessary job. Even I admit it's not on to leave a big pile of manure dumped in the middle of the yard!

An even better type of barrow, particularly for large yards or where one person is mucking out several boxes, is the four-wheeled type. These sometimes come with a special lever that tips the body up so it more or less empties itself, a boon if you are not particularly burly and this giant-size barrow is full. Two-wheeled barrows cost roughly £100 at the moment, four-wheeled ones more – but, yet again, they really are worth the saving in effort and time. And good tools well cared for last indefinitely.

Synthetic fabrics and other materials are normally much easier to care for than natural ones, an exception being yard brooms – the plastic bristled ones pick up every scrap of straw in their split ends! Natural bristle is best, and wooden handles are easier to hold, I feel. Wide-headed yard brooms are now available which have the advantage of sweeping more yard for the same amount of energy!

A field where synthetics really come into their own is that of horse clothing. New textile developments enable rugs to be multi-purpose these days; they are showerproof, in many cases, or even waterproof, yet still allow condensation from a wet horse to rise up through the fabric. Sweat and moisture can evaporate easily, which was never the case with the heavy old traditional New Zealand rugs. Gannex rugs were the first to meet these requirements, but nowadays there are several different fabrics which do the same job. The use of a mesh anti-sweat rug under one of these rugs enables a wet horse to dry off safely on a cold day, and this is especially useful in yards where straw bedding (for thatching) is unavailable because the horses are bedded on something else.

Not all synthetic rugs have this quality but even so they are, along with acrilan and other synthetic blankets and under-rugs, much easier to launder than the traditional jute/wool night rugs, heavy wool day rugs and woollen blankets of various kinds. You can bring a synthetic New Zealand rug home at night, wash it in the washing machine, dry it off in the airing cupboard overnight and have it ready for use next day.

Nylon web tack and harness are also increasingly popular: owners need only swish them clean in a tub of water, without having to do any laborious soaping afterwards, and can save their best leather tack for important occasions. Web tack of this kind is cheaper than leather (but ensure the fittings are rustless and of strong quality, which the best are) and very strong.

Improved plastics are also available for harness but users report problems with excessive sweating under it in some cases. Some people also believe that it is not strong enough to be used for driving. Synthetic saddles are now firmly established in the horse world with various designs, materials, colours and sizes. You simply have to give them a good brushing and hosing down to clean them.

Adjustable-tree saddles also save money for those with more than one horse or one whose work causes him to change condition significantly during the year due to seasonal work, putting on weight during summer and fining down again in winter if a hunter, and so on. These enable you to use one saddle for the same horse all the time or on different horses needing different width fittings as they can be altered by means of a key inserted at the pommel which you operate and can, by this means, obtain a precise fit for any horse.

We are all familiar with automatic drinkers, of course, and provided they are readily checked and have a drainage plug to facilitate cleaning out, they are good because they mean the horse always has water available. The plumbing has to be well lagged and protected, however, if the system is not to freeze in hard weather.

An added advantage of automatic drinkers is that you can have a meter so you know how much your horse has drunk, or otherwise. Water intake is a sign of general health or disorder, so an individual meter really is a good idea.

If, after thoroughly going through your equestrian obligations with a fine-tooth comb and finding you are still not managing or that you need more time with your horse, apply time management to other areas of your life. Try listing all your responsibilities, commitments and obligations and ask yourself whether you are not taking on just a bit too much. If your family are the old-fashioned type who believe one person in the family should be responsible for most of the domestic chores, and that person is you, re-educate them to take more care of each other and to do their share of the jobs. All but the youngest children are quite capable of keeping their own rooms clean and tidy without a parent chasing after them, for instance. Spouses, too, may take a bit of re-educating but can usually be brought to see that you are entitled to your horse and your own interests and that a shared home means shared work. Whoever makes the mess clears it up!

Domestic jobs can be prioritised and allocated on an A/B basis, just like horse jobs.

Take a look, too, at other aspects of your life. Do you sit on any committees? Do you have to sit on so many? Don't put yourself up for re-election next time if you want more time for your family, horse and friends. Try getting an answering machine at home so that when you really are too busy or too tired to get involved in a long gossip you can leave the machine on. More people will hang up than leave a message! On the other hand it could mean that, since you are out so much of the time, if a really important call comes through a message *will* be left so you will not miss it.

A valuable lesson to be learned in time management is how to say 'no'. In all walks of life there are people only too ready to delegate tasks they don't want to do, or to be responsible for, to someone who will. This is standard management practice – a manager should manage and supervise, not do. So try it yourself: delegate as many unimportant and distasteful tasks as you can on to someone else. If they won't accept, say gently: 'Well, that's a shame. I do understand how you feel, because that's how I'm fixed as well. I simply *can't* do the job in future because of personal and family commitments, so I suppose it will simply have to go by the board.'

Do not be inveigled into carrying on a job, 'just until we find someone else'. They rarely will. Simply give a month's notice, or whatever, and stick to it. Don't go into detailed explanations if they pry; you have already explained and the rest is none of their business. Say 'no' nicely, offer to spend a limited amount of time showing someone else the ropes and then pull the plug out.

Your time is your own, after all, and no one else's.

6 Organisation

Can you remember important points about your stable management or do you find yourself running things in a haphazard, hit-and-miss way? Wouldn't it be super never to be caught out – never to find that you can't go to a particular show or event because you didn't book the farrier in time and your horse's shoes are not in a fit condition, and never to look silly when your vet asks certain vital questions about your horse's work or diet and you are unable to answer accurately?

This is quite easy to achieve by creating your own personal planning system, which I call the 'master diary' system. It can be adapted for use by individual owners or by communal stables, and runs like this.

First buy an A4-size diary with one page to a day. Divide the days throughout the diary into three sections horizontally. The top one is your 'action' section for that day for reminders of jobs you must do, such as 'order feed', 'post entries for Bumpton one-day event' or 'get new spare wheel for trailer'. The middle section is for your horse's exercise and feeding programmes. Line this off vertically in three columns, the first for proposed exercise, the second for feed details and the third for remarks such as 'left 2nd feed, sluggish at exercise; temperature 39°C'. This gives a record of behaviour and food consumption to guide you for the future or to show your vet. During a long illness, records such as temperature, pulse, respiration and general behaviour including appetite can be vital.

The third horizontal section is your 'actual' section to record what actually happened on that day. If everything went as planned, note that; but if not, put what did occur, such as 'Tansy sick, vet came p.m. . . .' plus details of treatment. Note the quantities and names of drugs given for future reference. Also use this section to note things like 'farrier came p.m., two new front shoes, hind trimmed and reset, paid £X' or 'delivery of 24 bales paper bedding'.

Once the diary is ruled up, first put in it the information you wrote on your year planner such as your holidays, major shows or events and then minor ones. Your horse's fitness programme can then be worked out backwards from the dates of the main ones.

Also mark in the diary the dates of your horse's medicals, to be fitted round his work/holiday dates, vaccinations and boosters, teeth checks, blood tests or whatever is going to be done. Now, about two or three weeks before the diary entries, put a note in the action section to book the vet for the appropriate date. Mark on the date decided upon the approximate time that the vet will be arriving at the yard, so you can have the horse ready.

Ask the vet to help you plan the horse's worming routine and mark the appropriate dates for every worming throughout the year, making a note two weeks before to ensure that you have the drug in stock. Note the product used so that, if your vet advises it, a change to a different drug can be made so as to help avoid resistance in the parasites. If you have more than one horse, begin each entry with the individual horse's name so that you know at once to which horse it relates.

The fourth schedule you can put in the diary is your grazing care schedule – land treatment and rotation plan, soil tests, dates of fertilisers, which ones and in what amounts, etc.

At the end of the diary, mark any events/schedules/special dates to be carried forward to next year's diary, to make sure your programme carries on automatically.

When a regular task such as shoeing has been done, be sure to mark in the diary, say for two weeks later, to book the farrier again for three or four weeks after that. Then put down the date booked and the time, and which horses will probably need to be ready for him.

In a communal yard, it is an idea to get a diary with a hollow spine so you can thread some string down it, tie it to the table in the tack room and make sure it is never taken away. Owners can use it to enter when they are riding, when their horse should be seen to by someone else because the owner can't come, when the horse should be turned out, etc. It is also a good idea to have a pen or pencil on a string next to the diary.

If all owners get into the habit of looking at the diary, not to mention filling it in, every time they visit the yard, there will be little chance of mix-ups which could result in some poor horse not being fed or turned out. The manager or owner of the yard should write any messages left with her in the diary immediately, so that whoever is responsible for seeing to things that morning, afternoon or evening will know what has cropped up and can see to the horse in question.

If you use coloured pens for different subjects, say red for veterinary/worming entries, blue for farrier, green for shows, etc. you can see at a glance what is looming up in the near future – although a supply of pens like this might well 'walk' in a communal yard.

If you are responsible for more than two or three horses, you might also find it worthwhile to maintain a separate alphabetical card index system for each horse for things like shoeing, worming and veterinary treatments, plus accidents or any unusual happenings. You will then have a record by date in the diary and, in more detail, by individual horse on the index cards.

These index systems are readily available from stationers and office supply shops. They have plastic boxes with lids and alphabetical dividers (which will only be needed in very large yards) and include a supply of cards. For a small index, you can buy the cards separately and simply keep them in a polythene pocket taped inside the back of the diary.

Put the horse's name in the top left-hand corner of the card and keep the cards alphabetically so you can go straight to the relevant one. Also enter the horse's name, sex, year of foaling, breeding if known, the date he arrived in the yard and the owner's name, address and day and evening telephone numbers. Down the left-hand side rule a date column, and use the space on the right for entries, like this:

14 June	–	Farrier, 4 new. Corn pared out, off fore. Paid £X.
27 June	–	Wormed with Brand X.
1 July	–	Lame. Vet came. Rest as slight tendon strain.
	–	Cut out concentrates.

A second card can be filed behind the first for each horse, giving details of his fitness programme and diet plus the dates of any major competitions he attended. In this way, there is a ready record of the horse's management and activity available for vet, farrier or owner which can be most useful when illnesses or other disorders crop up in future.

Large yards will have separate shoeing records and 'communes' should have a feed chart, the latter normally being chalked up on a blackboard in the feed room.

With a thoughtfully planned, regularly updated diary and card index system like these, necessary tasks, appointments and accurate records unfold before you automatically on a daily basis. (The only problem is that you are sure to have a heart attack if you lose the diary!) Provided you have remembered to write everything in as a matter of habit every day, there is only one thing you will ever have to remember, and that is to *look in the diary*.

There are various organisers on the market if you don't want to create your own, some general and others specialised for different equestrian disciplines, and these enable you not only to organise your daily operations but also to keep records of whatever you wish to keep records of from vaccinations to show winnings.

You should keep careful records of your horse's registration numbers with different societies, the details of insurance policies with the policy numbers, premium payable and date renewable, and the dates your own subscriptions to various clubs and societies fall due. (Remember, if vaccinations are only one day overdue, you have to start again from scratch.)

The tack room should have a permanent list of useful telephone numbers, such as vets (at least two in case your usual vet cannot come), farrier, Riding Club secretary, Hunt secretary, saddler, feed merchant and hay/straw merchant if not the same. All owners' day and evening numbers should be on this list as well as the index cards, so there is a double record.

The Tack Room

Although I earlier said that tidying the tack room was a 'B' job in my book, there is a limit to the amount of disorganisation which should be allowed! An untidy mess with things not in their places could, in an emergency, cause a dangerous delay while searching for veterinary equipment. Also, it is obviously much more pleasant and satisfying when your belongings are reasonably clean and tidy. They are nicer to use and, because things well cared for tend to last longer, you save money too by being reasonably careful and tidy.

Fig. 14 Security and convenience in one. The Tack Safe, marketed by
Mr G. Asker, Kings Barn Farm, Medmenham, Marlow, Buckinghamshire, takes
two complete sets of tack, is of strong metal construction and, of course, locks
securely. Suitable for at-home or travelling use.

In a communal yard, with or without a manager, it may not be
that easy to keep things just as you would want them, but owners
should each be allocated a corner of the tack room for bits and
pieces, and their own numbered saddle and bridle places.

For such situations, I have found a free-standing 2 m (6 ft)
kitchen cabinet invaluable. These cabinets are usually lined with

easy-clean laminated board and have built-in baskets and trays which are ideal for plaiting equipment, veterinary supplies, grooming kit, bandages and suchlike. The lower halves usually have shelves and are quite roomy enough for storing rugs and blankets, a grooming machine, clippers and buckets. Some are even deep enough and big enough for you to fix a saddle rack inside and store your saddle, if you wish, and to put a bridle hanger (an empty saddle-soap tin) on the side or inside the door. Depending on the type of handles, you may be able to put a padlock and chain through them to keep your equipment where it belongs.

Tack rooms are used for storing leather items and so should have some sort of heating to keep the temperature at a reasonable level, about 20°C (68°F). Leather soon deteriorates in cold, damp conditions. The room can be used for drying off rugs and bandages, too. An old-fashioned rack consisting of four or more wooden or plastic poles hauled up above head height on a pulley is very handy for this. Patent rug holders which support the rug from its fastened breast strap are now available and are handy as they can fold flat against the wall when the rug is dry.

Saddle and bridle storage facilities should be available in sufficient number, and there are various types to choose from. Commercial makes can be obtained from saddlers, but a simple wooden upturned V-shaped structure supported at each end by floor-standing wooden sides can easily be made by a handyman. Saddles should not be stored on poles which fit between the seat panels as these stretch the webbing and seat leather and spoil the saddle. Bridles should be stored on rounded holders, such as old saddle-soap tins (as mentioned) or wooden semi-circles nailed to the wall, so that the headpieces keep their shape and do not become ridged and cracked as they do when simply hung on a nail or narrow peg.

For a single saddle and bridle, a short upturned V-shaped rack with one end nailed to a plank of wood, which in turn is nailed firmly to the wall, with a bridle holder fitted immediately underneath it, is a common and convenient way of storage.

A saddle horse is not essential for cleaning your saddle (which can be done by just resting it on your knee) but it is an asset. The most common sort usually have the upturned V structure mentioned above on a wooden stand and come to about waist height. There may be a boot shelf underneath and drawers for tack-cleaning equipment. The saddle is rested in the normal position on top for cleaning the outside, and then the V will usually turn over so that you can rest the saddle on its back inside the V to clean the underside. To clean the bridle you can, again, simply rest it on your knee or on the table, but your job will be made simpler if you use a proper bridle hook hanging from the ceiling. It should be put away after use (it should hook down from the ceiling easily) so that those in a hurry do not sustain head injuries on it – painful and dangerous, as many of us know!

In a large yard where an individual owner, or the owner of many horses such as a riding school, does not have individual facilities, there will need to be storage chests or cupboards for clothing, drawers for boots and bandages and shelves for the hundred-and-one things that seem to gravitate towards the tack room in any stable.

A clean, lockable cupboard should be available for veterinary supplies, and it is a good idea to have a list on the back of one of the doors stating what is in there. If any item is running low, it should be noted on another list and replaced before it runs out completely. A good veterinary book could be kept in the cupboard for reference, again with string threaded down the spine and tied down so the book is always where it is needed.

There should ideally be hot and cold running water in the tack room. At least there should be cold water, and either a kettle or a water heater. It is easier to clean grease off leather with slightly warm water, but *not* hot which can spoil and discolour the hide. In large establishments, there may well be washing machines and dryers in the tack room for rugs and blankets, not to mention jeans and working jodhpurs, anoraks and the like if these are not dealt with in the living quarters.

A tremendously useful facility in any yard, large or small, is a washing box with a neighbouring heater box for drying off. The washing box (or it could simply be an under-cover area, not an actual box) can have a hosepipe for hosing down horses attached by a screw fitting to a mixer tap which can be adjusted to give water at a variable temperature. Most people hose down horses with cold water which is, I feel, at the least unkind and would be regarded as cruelty in chilly weather if it were applied to humans (it is a standard means of torture, actually!). It is neither difficult nor expensive to install warm-water facilities in your yard and, without expensive plumbing, can be done simply by having put in an instant

(b)

(a)

(c)

Fig. 15 (a) Freeze-marking (here done by Equestrian Security Services) is carried out by means of the application of very cold marking irons to the horse's coat and skin. (b) A close-up of the code number on a horse freeze-marked by Equestrian Security Services. (c) Premises housing horses security freeze-marked by Equestrian Security Services can display this sign (in blue and white) provided by the company, to warn off potential thieves.

electric water heater of the type used for showers. Fit your hosepipe
to it and set the thermostat to horse's blood heat at 38°C or a little
warmer and you're away. No more chilled, miserable, reluctant and
maybe resistant horses but clean, warm, contented ones who
probably even enjoy their wash-down and, because they are warm,
will dry off quicker than if they were thoughtlessly done with cold
water.

A heater box for drying off is also a real boon and saves
thatching, rugging, leading round and so on. An infra-red heater in
the roof (mentioned earlier) is all that is needed. You just put the
horse in there with *no* rugs on, probably with the top door closed
but the window open, and a hay supply to keep him occupied, and
he will dry off very quickly, even with a long coat. Do not be
tempted to thatch him or rug him with a rug of any sort as he may
well overheat. In fact, if you rugged him with one of the heat-
retaining rugs you could well find that he actually burns under the
rug. The heater will keep him comfortably warm while he dries off
and the open window will ensure *some* air circulation.

It will greatly aid message leaving and receiving if your yard has
a telephone answering machine. This is not really extravagant:
second-hand ones are available from office equipment shops for
about £30. They are simple to operate and all owners in a
communal yard should learn how to work the machine and
transfer messages left on it to the diary. If the telephone and
machine are in a public place there may be fears on the part of the
yard manager/proprietor that people will be making calls at his or
her expense, but a lock can easily be fitted to the dial so that the
telephone is used for incoming calls only. A payphone (perhaps
portable) can be installed for outgoing calls.

Security

Some owners in a communal livery yard may feel it safer to take at
least their saddle and bridle home with them for safety's sake. Not
all yards have adequate precautions for tack security, particularly
the smaller, 'informal' yards, and there is a booming trade in stolen
tack and harness.

It is often advised that you mark your equipment with your post code but because there may be many people in your immediate vicinity with the same code you should end it with your house number or the first two letters of your house name. This, of course, is a nuisance when and if you move house because everything then has to be re-coded. A better system is to use your National Insurance Number which is yours for life, if rather long, or you could use the shorter number on your medical card.

Some of the companies which freeze-mark horses and ponies may also run a registration and marking scheme for equipment as well so it is a good plan to watch out for their advertisements in the horse press and contact them for details; other companies run equipment schemes without becoming involved in marking the animals themselves and new firms may emerge at any time which offer suitable security services.

The Police are an excellent source of general security advice and may know of regional or local security schemes, so contact the Crime Prevention Department of your local force.

As far as freeze-marking your horse or pony itself is concerned, again there is more than one company offering this service at present and there may be more in the future. Police forces and the British Horse Society fully approve of freeze-marking. The animal is marked wherever you wish but usually on the left side of the saddle patch so the mark cannot be seen when it is being ridden, with an exclusive, personal code number, by the application of super-cold irons which are held in place long enough to kill the colouring pigment in the skin so that hair regrows white in the shape of your number. For grey horses, the irons are held on longer to completely kill hair growth and the number is in bare skin. For horses who are wearing rugs, the company may supply sew-on or stick-on patches to deter thieves.

Freeze-marking has been extremely successful in not only restoring stolen or escaped animals to their rightful owners but in preventing theft in the first place. The marking companies usually offer a substantial reward to slaughterhouses and other people who are instrumental in giving them information leading to the successful conviction of a thief. The amount has to be well above meat price for the horse (as most animals are stolen to be sold on for meat) so that it is more worthwhile for those involved to report the horse than to put it through the auction. The Police *and* the marking company must be informed by anyone finding such a horse, or by the auction authorities.

Stolen horses can be slaughtered within hours – by the time you discover the theft, your horse could be dead – and slaughterhouses cannot possibly check on the legal ownership of every horse brought to them. With a freeze-marked horse, however, they know that if they ring the Police and the marking company to check on the animal's legal ownership (should it be offered for sale without its registration papers) they could end up with a good deal more cash than their commission on the horse's meat value.

The sale ring is a potential source of heartache for horse and pony owners. Once a horse has passed through a public auction with the status of a *Market Ouvert* (Open Market – which is most of them) the only way its original (rightful) owner can get it back is to buy it from the purchaser. This is the law, unjust though it seems, so having your animal freeze-marked can immediately alert the managers of the sale to check on its number and papers and to be suspicious if there are no papers or if the identity of the registered owner is not the same as the person offering the horse for sale.

Apart from freeze-marking, you can have your post code hot-branded on to your horse's front hooves by your farrier (you have to buy the irons from the company operating the registration scheme) and this will obviously have to be redone by him every six months or so as the horn grows out. The wall horn of a hoof is surprisingly thick at the toe and the brand is no detriment to the hoof. This method of marking is not so immediately visible as a white code number on the horse's back, of course, but is more acceptable to those who simply cannot bear the slight disfigurement caused by a freeze-mark.

Modern technology has also spread to the horse world in the form of electronic chip identity coding which has been used on other categories of animals for some years. A tiny microchip the size of a grain of rice is injected into your horse's neck by your veterinary surgeon. It bears, again, a personalised code number which is registered with the operating company. Scanners are made available at sales and to vets and the police so that a suspect animal can quickly be scanned and its identity and legal owner proved.

These and other schemes are regularly advertised and publicised in the equestrian press so it does pay to keep your eye on what is going on.

Police forces in some areas operate schemes similar to the now familiar Neighbourhood Watch schemes in rural areas. For instance, the Cheshire Constabulary pioneered their Countrywatch scheme aimed at encouraging all rural dwellers and users such as farmers, ramblers, villagers, commuters, fishermen, National Trust and wildlife park rangers and so on (obviously including those who ride and keep horses in rural areas) to become security conscious and report to them all suspicious incidents, taking notes of people and vehicles involved. Notices and stickers announcing the existence of such a scheme are known to reduce crime in a given area and such a scheme would certainly be well worthwhile joining or starting in conjunction with your local police force.

Apart from identity coding your horse in some way, it is advisable to take clear colour snapshots of him from both sides, front and back, with close-ups of any distinguishing marks or scars, and of each of his four chestnuts which are as individual to horses as our fingerprints are to us. It is true that a bit of 'surgery' can alter the appearance of chestnuts, but many thieves would not bother, so a record of the chestnuts is worthwhile.

Freeze marked or not, if your horse or pony *is* stolen or goes missing – perhaps taken by a joyrider and turned loose on the road or elsewhere – the people to ring immediately are the police and the coding company, confirming your telephone call in writing to the coding company at least. *Read the conditions set by the coding company very carefully and make sure you comply with them* as one company has been known to refuse to co-operate in finding a stolen horse because the owner did not confirm in writing or told the Police first!

You should have on hand the telephone numbers and names and addresses of all slaughterhouses and auctions in your region and enough copies of your photographs (which should clearly show the freeze marked code number on the horse's back) to send to them. The crime prevention department of your local police force and the other bodies already mentioned should be able to help you compile this list, and you can also use the Yellow Pages directory. Dealers should not normally accept a freeze marked horse for sale without supporting documentation, but ideally they, too, should receive details if your horse goes missing.

There is a tragic increase in the number of attacks on horses now. The attacks seem senseless and motiveless but, at the time of writing, press reports of horses being caused great suffering and

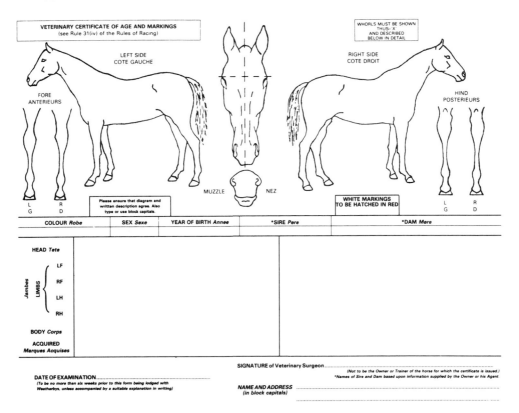

Fig. 16 In addition to freeze marking, it is advisable to have clear snapshots of your horse or to fill in an indentification form such as this, which is the standard veterinary certificate of age and markings required by Messrs Weatherbys (for the Jockey Club) used in recording Thoroughbreds and naming them under the very stringent Rules of Racing. It is the Jockey Club's policy and also that of Weatherbys, as proprietors of the General Stud Book in which all Thoroughbreds must be registered, to base their identification systems on natural marking factors, notably white markings and hair whorls. In certain difficult cases such as whole coloured bay animals, they sometimes ask that the chestnuts on all four legs are drawn to life size as they produce a unique identifying factor. They do not require any form of freeze marking for registration purposes but acknowledge that such marks are useful for identifying horses 'in the field' and as a deterrent against theft. (Reproduced by kind permission of Messrs Weatherbys.)

distress, and even death, as a result of vandalism are increasing. Freeze marking, of course, will not stop such attacks as the horses concerned are not stolen or even removed from their premises. Security of those premises is, therefore, a common-sense area for attention. The horses most at risk are those in isolated fields (maybe near roads, which give vandals easy access, but away from buildings, particularly inhabited houses) and those stabled (which make them easy to get at) in yards where there is no supervision for extended periods and/or where there are no living quarters for humans on the premises and which are, therefore, deserted for most of the time, especially at night.

The Horses and Ponies Protection Association recommend that all horses and ponies should be checked daily for injuries, signs of rugs having been removed and fitted differently (straps undone or fastened on the wrong side or twisted, etc.) and for bruising, wounding or discolouration under the tail. The horse should be studied for any unexplained mannerisms, and if you are in any doubt you are advised to call your veterinary surgeon. If you feel your horse has been tampered with, H.A.P.P.A. advise you to tell them and the police immediately.

Security of premises can obviously do a lot to prevent such attacks. It is true that if thieves or vandals really want to get into a place they will get in, no matter how good the security and whatever the premises, so the best we can do is make things difficult for them by effective security measures. Most thieves and vandals are opportunists – they will select the place which offers easy pickings rather than the one which will cause them problems.

It is an excellent idea to request a visit from your local crime prevention officer. The police are always ready to come and inspect your premises (at no charge) and tell you where security is weak and what you can do to improve it. They can recommend products and measures to help you foil unwanted visitors to your premises, and I have always found their advice practical and full of common sense. They won't say that your only hope is to install thousands of pounds worth of burglar alarms but will give you economical alternatives – maybe a cheaper burglar alarm. They will tell you what types of fencing, doors, locks, windows and so on to use, and will even suggest surfacing for paths (gravel, for instance, makes a noise when trodden on and would quickly alert a guard dog).

Basically, thieves and vandals can easily cope with wooden and wire fencing; thick, prickly hedging is much more difficult for them. If you can arrange it, have gates from the paddocks opening on to your premises rather than on to a public road. Make all gates the type which cannot be lifted off their hinges, and padlock and chain them securely at both ends.

Ideally, tack rooms should only be accessible from the house, although this might be impractical or, indeed, impossible where the house is not near the yard. In any case, tack room windows should have metal bars at them, not weak tubular rods or wood, and should have two different five-element mortise locks. The door should open outwards, not inwards, to make it difficult for it to shoulder in, and door and window frames should be very strongly fitted into the walls. If there is only one brick or stone building on the place, it is probably best to use it for tack and harness. This building should, ideally, not back on to a public highway.

A big guard dog – preferably two – with a bark to match roaming loose at night (but obviously with access to adequate, dry shelter) are a useful deterrent, but check the position with your crime prevention officer because even if the dogs bite someone who has actually broken on to your premises you can be held liable under current legislation, for their injuries. Geese, in fact, make excellent guards as they can be noisy and vicious without inflicting the same kinds of injuries as dogs, and are less prone to bribery with food!

If horses, stabled or out, are left with headcollars on they can easily be caught by thieves or vandals. This is one instance where a hard-to-catch horse or pony is a definite advantage. Horses in fields could well have their own protector in the form of a horse known to attack humans!

Having some kind of alarm bell or lighting system wired to the gate and/or fence surprises an intruder when he or she sets it off. This can be quite simply arranged with a car battery, a simple make-and-break contact and a strong light. Also have the light over the stable yard connected to a switch in the house so that the outside light can be switched on from inside. Security lights turned on by sensors whenever anyone approaches the property are now commonplace for houses and other premises and are very reasonable in price compared with the security they offer. Thieves hate being surprised, having their presence heralded and being able to be identified. It's true that many horses are taken in broad daylight, particularly from outlying fields and yards where no one actually lives, but you cannot cover every eventuality. All you can do is make life as difficult as possible for thieves who are then highly likely to go elsewhere.

It is also a good idea to get to know neighbours near your yard and paddocks and ask them if they would kindly let you know if strangers seem to be loitering or frequently visiting the area. Give them your day and evening telephone numbers, and give them at least a card at Christmas!

When you travel to shows and other events, do not leave your vehicle unattended ever and do not scatter tack and equipment on the ground where any passer-by can pick up an item and calmly walk off with it. Never leave the ignition keys in and certainly do not leave animals unattended – as is so often seen – tied up in the horsebox or trailer. Even in the stable area, it is preferable, if you can possibly arrange it, always to have at least one person watching the animals and equipment.

The British Horse Society produce a most useful leaflet on horse and tack thefts which they will send free (but an s.a.e. would be appreciated) to anyone requesting it, member or not.

The Feed Store

If it is to keep well, feed of all kinds must be stored properly. Mention has already been made of the necessity of keeping hay in a *dry* airy place as wet quickly leaches nutrients out of the hay and ruins it. Ideally, whether indoors, outdoors or half and half in an open-sided barn, it should be stored off the ground, although this may be difficult for large quantities. Wooden pallets are sometimes used for fairly small quantities; however, these permit rats to get under the fodder without being high enough to permit a cat or Jack Russell terrier to get underneath to root them out easily. A reasonable height would be 30 cm (1 ft), if this can be arranged. New hay should be stacked, if at all possible, with space between the bales; just a few centimetres make all the difference and allow the new hay to 'breathe'.

The feed room itself should have a dry atmosphere and should, as a matter of routine, be swept out as often as possible to avoid spilled food attracting rats and mice any more than is inevitable in farms and equestrian establishments. Hot running water, as for the tack room, is an advantage for making warm, damped feeds and for cleaning feed containers. If cooked feeds are going to be fed, a boiler will be needed in a large establishment or a hotplate in a small one. If your establishment cannot supply such a facility, you can always bring your own from home in a large camping-size vacuum flask.

Feed containers of whatever type should have painted on them the type of feed inside so there can be no mistakes. Horses' diets should be chalked up on a large blackboard and any changes inserted meticulously.

Much feed is wasted and many horses are incorrectly fed because their feed is not weighed out properly. This can result in overfeeding or underfeeding, so it pays from both an economic and a health point of view to have a method of weighing grain, coarse mix, nuts, etc. A large kitchen scale is quite adequate. Alternatively, a measure which holds a known weight of each type of feed used should be kept handy. It should have neatly marked on it, preferably painted on so that it cannot easily become obscured, the amount in weight of each feed used, so there is no 'a scoop of that'.

Hay or hay-age should also be weighed. If haynets are used, it is a simple matter to hang each net on a simple spring weigher, available from most tack suppliers or the better agricultural merchants. If hay is fed in racks or loose, weigh it by placing it on an opened-out sack, bringing the four corners together and hooking them on the weigher. The fodder can be carried to the stable in the same sack to help prevent bits blowing about the yard.

In large stables, a low, flat trolley is very useful to transport the horses' individual buckets round the boxes. Each box could have a number and a correspondingly numbered bucket should always be used for the occupant of that box. However, in cases where confusion is likely to arise, such as in yards with floating populations of horses and/or attendants, the horse's name should be on the box, if only on a temporary card inside a polythene envelope, and his box number should be put by his name on the feed chart in the feed room. Then someone who knows which horse is which should ensure that the right horse is in the right box!

Haynets do take a bit of time to fill, but the task can be made easier by aquiring an old-fashioned clothes horse and hooking the net on to the three points of the triangle it forms when open. Both hands can then be used to stuff the hay in and get the job done quickly and easily. The clothes horse can be used at other times for airing rugs and blankets or drying bandages, provided this does not prevent its being available in the feed room when required.

Present-day fire regulations may prevent you from storing hay in a loft above a stable block, as was commonly done during the first half of this century and before. Though an excellent space saving idea, it did result in many terrible fires. It may, however, be possible to do it today if you put in a fire-resistant floor to the loft. Your local fire department can give you full advice on this. They should be consulted about your premises in general, in any case, as hay and bedding are highly flammable and you must comply with fire regulations – not least the provision of adequate access for fire engines in case of a fire.

If you do have your hay stored 'on high' in some way, try to ensure the haulier has equipment to get it up there, otherwise you will have a very tiring and time-consuming job doing it yourself. It can also be a nuisance having to transport hay from the hay loft or barn to the horses. Lofts may have a chute or a simple hole in the floor, guarded by a trapdoor, down which the bales are simply dropped.

I learnt to ride, when very small, at a riding school based in one of these old stable blocks, and the trapdoor there opened into one of the stalls. The horse concerned, however, did not bat an eyelid, but simply stepped aside as each bale came down and took a good bite out of it before it was removed.

If a barn is some distance from the normal hay store or feed room in the yard, the flat trolley used for feed buckets can be used or, if you happen to have a farm cart and a driving horse or pony in your yard, you could press them into service – they would also be useful for carting jumps around the place. Otherwise, line the mucking-out barrow with clean sacks and carry the bales in that. Humans carrying individual bales is a very tiring and inefficient way to do the job!

Stable and Yard Layout

Most of us have little choice over our yard layout, particularly if we keep our horses at livery or in rented accommodation. Where we do have a choice, however, a little thought as to how the buildings are arranged can save a lot of time and work.

Any yard should be reasonably sheltered from prevailing winds. If there is no obvious prevailing wind, whatever shelter is available should be to the north and east, in Britain. In other countries, shelter should be on whatever side of the yard the coldest winds come from. Vast land masses are subject to extremes of temperature, so protection from winds blowing over them should be provided. Coastal areas are generally milder and less varying than inland regions.

Shelter belts such as trees, hedges or high, tough plastic mesh of small size will break the force of the winds rather than block them altogether as a brick wall would. The latter forces the wind over the wall and into the yard, often creating a tiny whirlwind which whips up whatever lightweight objects are in its path.

In a line of conventional modern loose boxes such as is often seen in British and Irish yards, it helps to have some kind of overhang roughly 2 m (2 yd) wide to protect the horses from rain or snow and from hot sun in summer. It is usual to have windows in these boxes on the same side as the door to prevent cross-draughts. However, in hot weather a cross-draught is a positive advantage, so windows should be provided on the back wall – or at least shutters or some other method (even just a removable plank of wood) of providing a welcome breeze in the box in summer.

It is normally recommended that such boxes face south so they get the sun most of the day. However, if windows or some other inlet for light is provided to the south, or there are roof skylights of some unbreakable material such as translucent polythene, this will be quite adequate and will allow the stables to be sited so that the horses have a good view of what is going on or so that their position is more convenient for the human attendants.

The American barn system of stabling is becoming increasingly popular. It is ideal in countries where extremes of temperature are experienced, as horses and humans can be protected from the weather nearly all the time. The barns have wide, often sliding, doors at both ends and the boxes are sited down the outside walls. The central aisle is usually wide enough to permit a tractor (or horse) and trailer to pass down the middle delivering feed, or removing manure which is often dumped out into the aisle for collection later.

The barn should be sited, if at all possible, so that it has one short end to the prevailing wind. This is so that in summer, when the end doors are left open, a cooling breeze can blow down the length of the barn but in winter, when the doors are closed, a comparatively small area is presented to the winds, so reducing their chilling effect. Here again, every opportunity should be taken to provide ventilation outlets such as ridge roof ventilators, extra opening windows or shutters high up on the walls and – a definite advantage from the horses' points of view – top-half doors in the outside walls at the back of each box so the horses can be allowed to look out in summer. In fact, full two-leaf doors can be provided to allow individual entrance to each box from outside. Apart from avoiding possible congestion in the centre aisle, this will provide another exit for each horse in case of fire or other emergency.

Other buildings can be converted for use as stables, of course, and indeed most owners have to convert rather than build to personal requirements. It is hoped that some of the accompanying illustrations will show suitable plans of accommodation and conversion ideas. Whatever method is used, an important point to remember is that the horses should have as much headroom as can be allowed. Many prefabricated loose boxes allow only 2.2 m (7 ft 6 in) to the eaves, which I feel is not high enough for either safety or ventilation. A 3.6 m (12 ft) eaves height should be aimed at wherever possible, to allow for a rearing horse. Lower heights are obviously acceptable for cobs and ponies.

Adequate floor space is also needed, and long narrow boxes should be avoided as they do not allow the horse to lie flat out in safety to sleep. Horses have an inbuilt need for space and a love of movement; they are not happy in confined stables and for this reason, although stalls are still in use in some establishments (and may be acceptable in those where the animals habitually get a great deal – several hours' – exercise each day), I cannot recommend them for privately owned horses, most of whom receive comparatively little exercise. Even when such a horse is turned out for several hours, I still feel that stalls are unacceptably restricting for most animals and can be very stressful to their occupants.

Generally speaking, a floor space of about 3.7 m x 4.3 m (12 ft x 14 ft) should be adequate for a horse of about sixteen hands high (more if he is of an active nature) and about 3.7 m x 3.0 m (12 ft x 10 ft) for ponies (a little less for small ponies).

A simple test of ventilation is to spend some time in the open air and then walk into an occupied stable. If you notice a significant difference in the air of the box, if it feels noticeably warm, stuffy or – worse – smelly, you can be sure that ventilation is inadequate.

It saves walking time if 'intermittent' little feed stores and tack rooms are sited at, say, every sixth box, whether indoors or out. In a long line of twelve boxes, for example, do not have feed/tack rooms at the far ends of the row but set them three boxes in from each end so that each one serves three stables on each side of it,

Fig. 17 Time can be saved by not having to enter a horse's box every time he
needs feeding. Hatches can be provided in the walls, like this, so that feed can be
tipped straight into the manger from outside, or, as in this case, from an indoor
corridor running down behind the row of boxes. Such a facility could be added to
an existing row of boxes, space permitting, by any reasonably competent
handyman, or be incorporated into a conversion or new building. A similar hatch
can be provided behind a hayrack so that hay can be stuffed into the rack from
the corridor and the hatch closed up again. Such corridors can be for human use
only and also, perhaps, for storage of such things as mucking out tools or, if
slightly wider and with a door of suitable dimensions in the back of the box, can
give an alternative exit/entrance for horses. The manger in this drawing is simply
the normal polythene type of corner manger (the safest as they cause no
projection for the horse to knock himself against) suspended in a metal frame
which is fixed to a wooden support in this case but could probably be fixed direct
to the wall of a wooden box. The manger has corner bars to facilitate lifting out
for cleaning, and also to prevent the horse wasting feed by scooping it up
the corners and out on to the floor.

Fig. 18 This drawing shows ideal facilities for yards large or small. The play area in the foreground was 'converted' from a boggy piece of ground by excavating and selling off the top soil, laying bricks, gravel and finally fine shale, providing a relatively dry, secure footing for the horses. They have a shelter with haynets, which is kept on deep litter bedding. The door in the back allows easy access for humans but the horses are brought in through the gate on the left. Water is provided by hosepipe to the plastic dustbin tied to the fence and rammed into an old tractor tyre for security. If the gate to the field on the right is left open, the horses can come and go as they wish; there is no need to provide another shelter in the field as they can always get to the one in the play area. When ground conditions are bad, the gate is closed and the horses restricted to the play area/shelter complex, which they prefer to being kept stabled. Note how the fence between field and play area has had a single rail at horse's shoulder height run along on the field side, for safety. This small establishment shows how imaginative thinking and consideration for the horses can provide ideal facilities for the benefit of horses and humans.

reducing the distance the attendants responsible for those boxes have to travel.

Time can also be saved by having mangers and hay holders sited on the outside walls so that they can be reached by opening a hatch and the food can be put in without the door being undone, the horse dodged round and the door fastened again. It is surprising how much time this facility saves when you have a lot of horses to feed.

Where horses are yarded, such hatches make the filling up of communal hayracks much easier. There is no need to remove sliprails or open gates, fight your way through a small herd (even two!) of horses grabbing at the hay before you have had a chance to put it in the racks and then retrace your steps again. Yarded horses, however, may need concentrates feeding separately to ensure that each one gets his correct ration and, although this may be difficult to arrange, the yarding system saves so much time and work in other respects that it is not a serious disadvantage. Yards with shelters (run-in sheds) can conveniently be made to continue on into the paddock or field (pasture), so avoiding the need for a shelter in the paddock as well. Depending on the exact position of the shelter, it is useful to humans to have access into it for themselves and for the horses from the stable yard, and also to have some means (probably strongly constructed gates or sliprails) of keeping the horses in the shelter itself without access to the yard/paddock, perhaps in cases where either is waterlogged due to excessive rainfall. Left to themselves, most horses will spend much of their time outside in yard or paddock rather than where we think they should want to be – in the shelter. However, if the shelter is big enough the horses will still be happier in there together than stabled individually.

For paddocks with simple field shelters in them, one shelter can, with a little imagination and depending on the exact layout of your premises be made to serve three paddocks or more. The same goes for watering points. However, shelters still have to be skipped out and stocked up with hay and the horses caught up and inspected at least twice daily, so it is more convenient and time saving to have the shelters as near as is reasonably possible to the yard to cut down distances for carting hay/bedding and other gear to and fro.

7 Care of the horse

The purpose of this book has been to discuss how to look after horses spending as little time and money as possible. While speaking on this subject at a seminar before the book was finished, it was pointed out to me that it is all very well cutting corners if you know exactly where to cut them without harming the horse or compromising his welfare. To do this, you need to be a knowledgeable horsemaster. Advising novices to cut down on certain tasks could, it was suggested, lead to important areas of management being skimped due to lack of understanding. It is like learning to recognise injury or illness in a horse: how can we know what is abnormal if we do not know what is normal? It is because of this suggestion that this final chapter on basic care and management has been included.

There are many books on how to look after horses and ponies, and they are all slightly different due to their authors' having slightly differing opinions on various aspects of the subject. One of the best books on general horse care and management available at the time of writing is *Horse and Stable Management* by Jeremy Houghton Brown and Vincent Powell-Smith, published by Blackwell Scientific Publications. It is more advanced than most management books and covers, in an easily understandable way, topics often only discussed in veterinary books for horse owners.

The following discussion of the most important aspects of basic care and management of the horse inevitably comprises my own knowledge and opinions on the subject gained over many years of practice, observation and study. I hope it will be useful to readers in helping them to decide where to cut the corners mentioned earlier, so enabling them to care properly for their animals while saving both time and money. It will also add further comments on the main theme of the book – saving time and money.

The days are long gone when yards could provide one groom per two or three horses. The economics of horse keeping in the latter part of the twentieth century preclude the continuance of many of the practices devised by the employers and managers of the nineteenth century (many of whose methods live on in present-day textbooks and establishments where 'traditional' ways persist). There simply isn't the time and money to perform some of them and, fortunately for the working horse owner or any owner who hasn't all day to devote to his or her horse or horses, there are many tasks which can safely be skimped or skipped without any harm to the horse.

Some of the ideas and methods I recommend may seem like sacrilege to purists and traditionalists, but they have withstood many years of practice with no detriment to the many different types of horses and ponies involved.

Psychology and Physiology

The horse is a herd animal and an animal of the wide open spaces. Most members of the horse family (and this includes asses and zebras as well) do not do well either mentally or physically when living alone. There are odd exceptions but most equidae thrive on company. Similarly, most of them do not do well when kept confined. Horses are not cave dwellers like apes (human apes, anyway) and do not live in dens like dogs. They are, by natural evolution, nomadic within a certain territory. They have a natural love of and need for space, company, movement and an all-round view; life in a stable is highly unnatural to them, and too much of it certainly causes problems, both mental and physical.

Many of the stable vices we normally attribute to boredom can in truth be blamed accurately on the frustration and distress of over-confinement. Although a horse really confirmed in a particular vice may be difficult or impossible to cure completely, most horses I have come across improve tremendously when managed in a more natural manner. And not only do vices of various kinds lessen or disappear: their temperaments improve where they have previously been suspect or downright nasty, and the sad yearning so apparent in many stable-kept horses, and the dull resignation shown by just as many others, are replaced by a very obvious air of happiness and calm contentment. The horses are also much more interested in life in general, more amenable to their human handlers and more willing in their work.

I am not advocating that all horses should be 'freed of their shackles', as it were, and kept permanently at grass with all the disadvantages this entails for both horse and owner. What I do know, however, is that horses become much easier and pleasanter to look after when they are happy and, from a working owner's point of view, the work involved in their care is lessened by keeping horses in a manner suited to their mental as well as their physical needs.

We all know that one of the most often quoted rules of feeding is 'feed little and often' to follow the horse's natural way of taking in and digesting food. We make an effort to meet his needs in this respect, but many of us appear to overlook completely his needs with respect to mental health and happiness which are so easily met by turning him out into a grass paddock for some time each day, allowing him a reasonable amount of freedom. If grass is unavailable, freedom and the chance to do as he likes for a period can be provided by turning him into a prepared riding area such as an indoor school, outdoor manège or just one of the play areas already mentioned.

To do the job properly, he should be with another horse or pony with whom he gets on well. This turning-out period should be regarded as of equal importance to other daily requirements such as feeding and mucking out and, certainly, as ridden or driven exercise. Horses may certainly enjoy the work we ask them to do and many, in fact, feel left out and neglected when not in work, but exercise under constraint is not a substitute for liberty.

The provision of liberty needs adequate facilities, but, as suggested, it should not be beyond the means of most yards to provide them, using a little imagination.

Of course, even hardy cobs and ponies are not happy confined to an exposed field, offering no real shelter from driving rain, wind, sun and flies, for long periods, especially if they are alone. In truly natural conditions, animals do have the chance to find natural shelter; trees, shrubs and hills all help break the worst force of the weather and offer some shade in summer.

Natural social contact is also much more important than many owners seem (or wish) to acknowledge. Horses feel more secure in the company of their own kind. In the wild, when herds were subject to predators (as they still are in some parts of the world), there was safety in numbers. If there are a lot of you running together, the predator will be spoilt for choice and, with luck, will

pick someone else for dinner. This need for company is very strong
in horses, domesticated or feral, although some do seem to survive
contentedly alone. However, my experience of those formerly kept
alone is that they almost invariably prefer company when given a
choice.

Even stallions usually turned out alone are better when they can
see other animals around them. Those who habitually run with
their mares have a much more balanced, calm and natural outlook
on life than those used solely in hand and never allowed to
associate naturally with their own kind: stallions who are turned
out with an elderly, experienced, non-breeding female companion,
even if they serve their 'proper' mares in hand, again have a much
happier and sensible outlook on life than those deprived of what is,
in effect, their birthright.

It is obvious, therefore, that the opportunity to move around at
liberty, even in a small paddock or a dirt play area, for a few hours
a day is far better than being confined to a stable too much of the
time. Two friends can be turned together into even quite a small
area and will exercise each other and be company, too. Most yards
have the odd unused area, or could sacrifice some space
somewhere – preferably adjoining a loose box or with some kind
of shed in it – which could be converted into such an area.

The top soil (if the area is earth) could be sold or used elsewhere
on the premises and the area laid down with bricks and
subsequently covered with some suitable material, such as fine
gravel, and topped with used bedding (minus droppings), clinker,
shale or something similar. Such a facility can be a boon to any
establishment but particularly to a working owner short of time for
exercising or, indeed, to anyone who believes, as I do, that horses
are better off with as much liberty as is reasonably possible.

Yards of this kind are invariably useable when paddocks are
simply too muddy, or can be used to save the grass or to give
horses some sense of freedom without their getting filthy and
creating the extra job of cleaning them up. Just a few hours a day
in such a yard in addition to normal exercise can make our job that
much easier by keeping the horses saner and happier than most are
when confined to their stables except at working times. As the
horses will spend most of their time in the yard from choice, their
stable beds are saved, soo, making less work for us and less
expenditure on bedding material.

Even just moving about slowly is better for the horse's physical health than being kept stabled and standing still for the very long periods to which many horses are subjected. Horses normally prone to filled legs, for example, simply do not seem to get them when given small play areas like this, because of the benefit to the circulation. And, of course, the fresh air is of undoubted benefit, even to horses not prone to respiratory allergies to such things as stable dust (even in apparently well ventilated stables).

It is, therefore, an advantage to the horse and to his busy working owner if a little thought can be brought to bear on the subject of facilities for liberty and company.

Fencing is, of course, important in providing any sort of enclosure and its cost is one reason why facilities are so often lacking. The best way of keeping horses in their place, as it were, is to surround their paddock with thick, high, non-toxic, prickly

Fig. 19 A natural hedge in the process of being laid. This photo was taken by Hugh Laxton during the National Hedgelaying Competition in February 1983 and is reproduced by kind permission of the British Trust for Conservation Volunteers. The branches are laid diagonally, as shown, against supports. The bark is left on the lower side of the branches so they will not die, but continue to grow.

Fig. 20 A finished hedge, showing a neat, strong, professional job. This hedge will provide a 'living wall' which will be very difficult for any stock to penetrate. It should be left higher for horses than cattle and trees can be left in the hedge for an added windbreak. The hedge should be fenced off, perhaps with just a single strand of wire or flexible fencing (which can later be used elsewhere) to stop the horses eating it for two years while it matures. Thereafter, it should require little or no attention for many years, with the exception of judicious, knowledgeable trimming perhaps every three years. Hedging of this type is ultimately far cheaper and more trouble-free than any man-made fencing. It also forms a valuable windbreak and adds to the appearance and ecology of your area. (This photo is reproduced by kind permission of the Agricultural Development Advisory Service Unit of the Ministry of Agriculture, Fisheries and Food.)

hedging. This clearly cannot be provided overnight or even in less than a matter of years but, if the land is your own or you have it on a long-term lease, it certainly pays to grow hedging. Once mature, it requires very little maintenance – trimming (but not butchering) about every two years encourages thick, healthy growth, and having the hedge professionally laid when it has reached maturity makes it stockproof for many years to come. It is better from a conservation and wildlife point of view and also from the point of view of easier future maintenance to grow your hedges into a flat-topped A-shape so that they are thicker at the bottom than the top.

For horses, hedging should be higher than it is for cattle; it should be at least the height of the horses' backs, but if you want your hedging to make a really effective windbreak you can have it a good 2 m (6 ft) high. A thickness of about 60 cm (2 ft) will make for security and will thwart both horses, Houdini-type ponies and intruders. Your hedge will also provide very much needed habitat for wildlife and a 'highway' system for animals and birds, enabling them to spread their area, thus giving them a better chance of survival in our over-intensively farmed country.

The next most popular and suitable fence for horses has traditionally been timber posts and rails, although close-boarded fencing, which consisted of planks of timber set upwards and immediately next to each other allowing the horse no view out, was and still often is used on studs for stallions. Close-boarded fencing is now prohibitively expensive for any but large establishments where economy is not a significant priority. It is not essential these days, anyway, as other alternatives, such as diamond-mesh wire fencing bordered by timber and supported by timber posts, are now available.

Post and rail fencing can be quite expensive, too, but economies can be made where it is to be used for mature horses. Here, two-rail fencing is quite adequate, with the top rail at horse's back height and the next about half way between it and the ground. On studs, three and probably four-rail fencing will be needed to stop foals getting through the fencing or rolling near it and ending up, panic stricken, away from mum on the other side. In such cases, the bottom rail should be about 30 cm (12 ins) from the ground.

Perhaps the most commonly used and popular – because of its relative safety and economy – fencing for horses is plain, heavy-gauge wire on wooden or concrete posts. Provided it is kept tightly strained, it is a fair fencing. Should one strand give way for any reason, however, it will sag along the whole of its length, lowering the fence if it is the top strand. Whichever strand it is, it will leave swathes of loose wire about for the horses to get tangled up in – and they probably will. With a shod horse, there is also some chance that, should he paw the wire or be larking about near it, a wire could become wedged between the heel of the shoe and the hoof, creating a panic-stricken horse which injures itself in its struggles to get free (either by ripping off the shoe or severely straining tendons, ligaments or muscles) and a damaged fence.

Where such fencing is used, wire clippers should be kept handy – and always in the same place when not in use so that everyone knows where to find them in an emergency.

Square or rectangular mesh fencing is widely seen, from ordinary agricultural sheep-netting which is lethal to a type specially made for horses with smaller meshes near the bottom, ostensibly small enough to prevent a horse getting a foot through but in practice and my experience not effective in this regard and I cannot recommend it.

Diamond small-mesh fencing is making its appearance from the USA and is excellent – not the weak, wobbly, plastic-covered sort used in so-called 'security' fencing which almost anyone can break through by either cutting or unravelling it, but tough, taut complex diamond-shaped mesh on wooden frames, and this seems very good, used extensively, as it is, on thoroughbred studs.

Wire (and sometimes electrified) dropper fencing is also quite good; here the posts are even further apart as droppers (metal tubes with holes in) are set at various heights and distances along the wires to facilitate the straining. This type of fencing also has the advantage that, should a strand give way, only the section between two droppers will collapse, so lessening the effect.

Flexible-rail fencing is also used for horses now, the wire-reinforced sort being the most hard-wearing. The rails are made of a synthetic material which comes on rolls or in sections to be nailed to timber posts. I like this type of fencing for working owners, because you can use it to reinforce existing fencing which needs mending before your horse can go out but, when and if you leave that particular place, you can take it with you. For example, if you have rented a field from a farmer for the summer but the fencing is either hopelessly inadequate or, worse, dangerous because it is barbed wire (an absolute no-no for horses), you can buy the required amount for a single level of this fencing and fasten it to the tops of the existing posts, then simply take it down when your rental period is over – perhaps using it elsewhere or keeping it for emergencies.

Unfortunately, many barbed-wire fences are barbed on all their strands, and these are quite unsuitable for horses who may get a leg over a lower strand with disastrous results. Some farmers, however, simply use barbed wire for the top strand, so you could use your flexible fencing inside it.

Another kind of portable fencing is, of course, heavy-gauge

electric fencing. It has been used successfully for horses for many years, but not everyone likes it. The portable type will be supported usually on metal rods stuck into the ground; it is best used a little way inside existing fencing which is either dangerous or inadequate, to keep horses well away. For a slightly more permanent arrangement but one which you can still take with you, fix insulators to take the wire on the tops of existing posts and run your wire through them to the battery or mains supply, as the case may be, so that it becomes electrified.

Another form of electric fencing resembles a shiny metal ribbon, sometimes with brightly coloured plastic strips or 'flashes' on it so that horses really can see it (they can't always see ordinary wire).

Horses should be correctly introduced to electric fencing. Damp their noses, lead them up to it and press their noses against the wire. They should receive enough of a shock to send them sharply

Fig. 21 An example of flexible fencing. This is Caledonian Stud Rail marketed by Caledonian Fencing Ltd of Phoenix Works, North Street, Lewes, Sussex. Flexible fencing, especially the wire-reinforced type like this, is both useful and economical. It can be fairly easily taken down and used in a new location on existing posts, either as a single rail to reinforce broken fencing, as full fencing on its own, to mask barbed wire or repair odd lengths of other fencing. It is also useful for running a single length of white rail in a foal or youngstock paddock to provide an 'eyeline' to ensure the youngsters see the fencing when charging about. The fencing is shown here in a stud situation where four rails have been used. For mature horses, two rails are quite adequate, the top rail at the height of the horse's backs and the second at the height of their elbows.

back without actually being hurt. Lead them all along the electric fencing, repeating the operation at intervals, and you should soon find that when you try to get them to 'sniff' the fence they refuse point blank.

Unfortunately, there is a disadvantage as reported in a reader's letter to one of the equestrian journals. The reader had a young horse grazing within electric fencing. He swished his tail near the fence and the hairs became wrapped round the wire, obviously giving him a shock in the tail. The horse panicked and, his tail still round the wire, galloped off pulling the fencing round the paddock with him. Fortunately, the owner was nearby and saw what happened, and all that resulted was a badly frightened horse. This could certainly be a problem with the type of electric fencing which is only supported by metal rods pushed into the ground. However, with the more permanent type, particularly if used for the top strand of a fence as it should be, the likelihood of such a thing happening should be small.

Probably the most expensive form of fencing, in terms of both money and time for maintenance, is white-painted post and rail fencing. Peeling white paint looks terrible so it has to be redone regularly if you want it to look top notch. And in fact, from an ecological point of view, white fencing is an eyesore, a blot on the landscape which I feel we can well do without in every way.

Preserving the timber parts of your fence is obviously very important. Creosote can be poisonous to horses, a fact not always appreciated by those who daub it on with the very best of intentions. Modern preservatives are safe and most fencing suppliers and contractors supply timber already treated with either their own make of preservative or their favoured product. They can give you advice on looking after your timber after erection, too.

A point against any timber, whether it is hardwood or softwood, is that some horses *will* chew it. Horses often do this if they are short of bulk (such as when the grass is poor) or when they are bored (again, when the grass is poor because, especially in a small area with no other food laid on and perhaps no company either, they simply have nothing else to do). Young horses might chew a fence when teething and, although this is a temporary phase, it can last quite a long time – long enough for them to weaken and ruin the appearance of the wooden rails.

Running wire, especially electrified wire, along the top rail (the one most convenient for them to grasp) often stops the practice, but it might be considerate to provide young horses with a 'teething post', such as I once saw on a top Thoroughbred stud, in one corner of the field where they cannot bump into it.

Fencing posts should be sunk into the ground for two-thirds of their length at least; when you remember that an average riding horse can easily weigh half a tonne, it does not take much imagination to realise what can all too easily happen to an improperly sunken post, and what will then happen to the attached fencing. Wobbly posts also make fence repairs and general maintenance difficult or impossible, so don't economise on the length of posts. Whatever your expenditure on fencing, it should be regarded as an essential facility to enable your horse to be turned out, easing the time/work burden on you. The most economical type of fencing compatible with your needs and preferences should be used.

A point to make about any fencing is that the rails (wooden or flexible) or wires should be on the *inside* of the posts, as the idea is not only to present as smooth a barrier as possible to galloping horses (so they do not sustain injuries on the posts, usually at the shoulder) but to prevent the rails or wires being pushed off the posts by leaning horses. If a single fence is used to separate two fields, a single rail/wire at point-of-shoulder height should be run on the side where the posts are 'exposed', for the reasons just given. Ideally, also, corners should have a rail set across them to 'round' them off and steer galloping horses round the corner, not into it. Sharp (acute) corners should never be used for horses as one can easily hem in another during a kicking match and the one with no escape could be seriously injured.

Feeding

When horses are able to eat at their leisure – as when in a paddock with ample grass on it – they tend to spend about sixteen hours a day nibbling grass and/or browsing on leaves from trees, shrubs and hedges. Vegetation such as this is their natural food, but it is fibrous and bulky and they need to eat a lot of it to obtain the nourishment they need. Therefore they have evolved to eat more or less continuously and always to have a little food passing through their digestive tract.

This system is in direct contrast to that of their hunters in the wild, carnivorous animals such as those of the cat and dog families. These hunters live on meat, which is a highly concentrated food, and have evolved to eat (when they can make a kill) one large meal all at once, often making it last them for several days. Carnivorous animals have, therefore, very large stomachs compared to herbivores, like horses, which have small stomachs and long digestive tracts to cope with a little fibrous food passing through continually.

Digestion starts in the mouth. The front teeth (the incisors) crop off grass and leaves, and the grinding teeth at the back (the molars) crush the food up. The tongue manipulates it all and helps it to become mixed with saliva which contains mild chemicals that prepare the food for the stronger digestive juices it will encounter in the stomach.

The horse's stomach works best when two-thirds full (including both food and digestive juices). The food is mixed with digestive juices here, and passes on down the digestive tract or intestine, which is a long, compartmentalised tube with muscular walls that push the food ever onwards in a wave-like movement called 'peristalsis'. In the gut the food is mixed with other digestive juices and microscopic bacteria which help process the food; the various nutriments in it are absorbed into the blood and lymph vessels through the gut walls and are then passed on to the various parts of the body needing them, being first 'filtered' by the liver which removes many harmful substances, changes them into harmless ones and excretes them again in the bile in an unabsorbable form, helping protect the body against poisons, etc. (In cases where very potent poisons, such as ragwort, are eaten, the liver cannot cope and becomes seriously damaged, affecting its many other functions and causing serious illness or death.)

The nutrients excess to immediate requirements are stored in various 'depots' around the body – the liver being one – for later use. The more food that is stored, of course, the fatter the horse gets. Horses fed too little for their requirements obviously lose weight, as there is not only insufficient to store but insufficient to meet current needs. When a horse is starved, his body actually uses up its own tissue, particularly muscle, (hence the descriptive phrase 'skin and bone') and the horse becomes emaciated.

Food is used for the production of body tissue such as muscle, skin, bone, horn, etc., maintaining the body's temperature at around 38°C (100.4°F), putting on condition (storage of food as just described) and providing energy for work or just for the very processes which keep the horse alive such as heartbeat, hormone production and digestion itself.

If a horse reaches the stage of being so thin that he is using up all his own body tissues then obviously all the other requirements are affected; there is simply not enough fuel to keep the horse's body going, and death can result. Conversely, when there is far too much food taken in for the body's requirements, such as when a horse is over-fed and under-worked by us or turned out for a rest on over-rich grazing, he will not only become fat but may develop serious and sometimes fatal circulatory and digestive problems like colic and tying-up or set-fast (often called azoturia).

Feed constituents are varied and most feeds contain several types. The constituents are: proteins, carbohydrates, fats, water, vitamins, minerals, trace elements and fibre.

A horse can survive very much longer without food than he can without water. Fresh water is, after air, the world's most vital resource and lack of it leads to dehydration and many other problems. Dehydration can occur in winter, when horses' water sources are iced over, as well as in summer. It is always stressed that supplies should have the ice broken and taken out of the container because horses usually do not break the ice themselves and many are put off drinking, even when quite thirsty, by broken ice floating on the top of a trough.

A horse's body can consist of about 70% water (the younger the horse, the more water his body contains). The cells of the body are surrounded by and contain water-based fluids, and even horn and hair contain it. Blood is, of course, mainly water, as are lymph and the digestive juices; the eyes contain water and the horse's joints are lubricated by a fluid called synovia. Mares obviously use water to make milk, and the horse's excretory systems depend on fluid – urine transports waste products out of the body, droppings are moist and sweat contains waste products. The sweat is also important to regulate body temperature. Heat is lost by the evaporation of warm sweat into the surrounding air.

As water has so many different uses in the body, dehydration can clearly be a very serious condition.

All the normal feeds we give our horses contain some water, and of course grass contains a relatively large amount. However, an additional supply is needed: ponies and horses can drink anything from six to fifteen gallons (27–68 litres) a day depending on size,

Fig. 22 This type of feed container is ideal for field or stable use. It is one of the Kanguro range marketed by Messrs Faulks & Jaques of 27 Innage Park, Holly Lane, Atherstone, Warwickshire. The features of the range are that they are almost indestructible, being of very tough yet soft material which can be run over by a Land Rover or kicked about by a horse without being spoiled or broken. As they are not rigid, they will not crack and will not injure a horse should he tread or lie on them. Their durability makes them very economical in use.

Fig. 23 The Kanguro range of feed containers, buckets and dung skeps.

work and weather. If he is short of water, a horse's body will draw on its own fluids and this can result in dehydration.

Water is even lost from the body in the water vapour from the lungs when the horse breathes, and this continual use and loss makes an adequate supply essential at all times. Horses working hard in hot conditions are particularly prone to dehydration, especially those whose work is prolonged such as endurance horses and three-day event horses.

In the wild, equidae normally drink early in the morning and in the evening, when possible, often trekking long distances to water holes. Zebras in southern Africa have been said to go regularly for three days or so without drinking, apparently without suffering significantly. However, this is not the sort of lifestyle we would want our domesticated horses and ponies to experience, and most books on management recommend that water is always available to the horse in stable and field.

Even today, there are establishments which water horses morning and night, and after work (before feeding) – usually military and police establishments. This is a job in itself, either carrying water to the horses or taking them to drink from a communal trough (not the most hygienic of practices), and much time and work is saved by having automatic waterers in the stables. Here, the horses can drink a little whenever they wish. People who say horses should have their water removed before feeding do have a point, but it is my experience that horses who have water always with them do not take a long draught even straight after work.

Some horses do like to drink immediately after and sometimes even during feeding, but again I have found this is not harmful provided the water is always available, resulting in small amounts being taken as normal. It is now felt that this actually stimulates the digestive juices and helps, rather than hinders, digestion.

A point about ordinary automatic waterers is that you cannot tell how much or how little a horse is drinking. As water intake is a valuable sign of health and disease, it is worthwhile seeking out the type of waterer which has a small meter attached so you can see at a glance how much is being used. Also, a good type of appliance is one with a plughole at the bottom so that it can easily be drained and cleaned. The type of plug with a little inset handle is impossible for the horse to pull out.

Horses are not generally happy with the nose-operated cattle-type of waterer, where they have to press down a lever to get water. The method where the container automatically fills up as the horse drinks is preferable.

Water can also be supplied in buckets, of course. Any bucket used should be of soft plastic for better wearing qualities; these are also less likely than metal or rigid plastic buckets to injure the horse should he tread or lie on them. Wooden buckets are a job in themselves to keep sweet and clean, whereas plastic buckets need only a simple daily scrub-out with an old dandy or water brush.

Particularly at night, a horse should be left with two buckets of water rather than one. If you regularly put them in the same two different corners, the horse will always know where they are in the dark and, should he do a dropping in one, the other will still be clean for him to drink. If the two buckets are next to each other, the dropping will invariably go into both of them.

Horses in fields are often left with a stagnant pond for water, which is quite unsuitable. Streams and ponds these days are quite likely to be polluted, so regular testing (consult your vet or agricultural adviser) is recommended. It is said that, over a period of time, horses drinking from streams with sandy bottoms can develop sand colic, so gravel or stony bottoms are preferred.

I feel it is very difficult to find a safe pond and that in general ponds are better fenced off and left for the wildlife. Horses and ponies can not only slip into them on unsafe approaches, but can wander on to the ice in winter with fatal results.

Incidentally, if a horse consistently prefers muddy, seemingly unclean water to fresh, it could be a sign he is short of minerals in his diet.

Troughs can form very satisfactory water containers with a little thought. Some people stock them with fish to keep them clean (although this has been known to frighten the horses initially!) and, in any case, a regular clearing-out operation should take place to check for debris such as leaves and dead birds. The supply should be checked twice daily to see that the trough is neither empty nor overflowing due to a malfunction of the ball-cock system, and all 'moving parts', taps and other mechanisms should be securely covered with metal or wood to stop horses interfering with them.

Where laid-on water is unavailable, perfectly adequate watering sources can be provided by plastic dustbins rammed into tyres (this idea can also be adopted for buckets in stables) and tied by the handles to the fence posts. They can then be filled by hosepipe from any nearby tap. Remember to keep the level high and to bring the hose indoors in frosty weather for if the water inside it freezes you are, effectively, without a hosepipe until it thaws.

Large plastic water tanks such as are used in house and garden situations can also be used here. Rigid plastic is subject to cracking if the horses decide to chew it, or in hard weather and even in strong sun, so softer materials are normally longer lasting. Moveable water sources like this have the advantage that they can be moved down one post each day so that the surrounding area does not become badly poached, as often happens with fixed troughs. The latter do have the advantage, however, of being able to serve two fields by being set into the fence so animals on both sides can get at them.

Do not set water containers actually in a corner as this can encourage escape problems if two or three horses are jostling to drink at the same time.

Carbohyrates are the starches and sugars in the diet; most grain feeds such as oats and barley are mainly carbohydrate, as are coarse mixes and cubes. Carbohydrates produce energy and heat and excess intake is stored as fat in the body. Carbohydrate is also found in grass, particularly coarse grass and hay/hay-age, and in popular additives like molasses/black treacle and honey. Sugar-beet pulp is rich in carbohydrate, as are fodder beets which are usually only easily come by in the south of Britain.

Proteins are the only foods able to manufacture body tissues such as skin, muscles, organs and so on. Excess protein can be stored, although some is excreted by the kidneys. However, when it is stored it loses its tissue-building properties; therefore, a daily supply of protein is needed for health. Apart from this 'building' function of protein, it can also provide heat and energy.

Most foods contain some protein; many of the carbohydrate sources also contain protein (oats, barley, hay, grass, etc.) although in lesser amounts. Spring grass is rich in protein and too much can have serious digestive and circulatory effects on horses, so care should be taken when introducing horses to this type of grazing. It should be done in very short spells, starting with half an hour and limited to probably about a couple of hours a day, depending on individual conditions.

If a protein supplement or boost is felt to be needed, as with a very thin horse or backward foal, the foods people tend to think of are high-protein cubes or coarse mixes. Beans and peas are noted for their protein content but are not often used these days; special protein supplements might be recommended by your vet or nutritionist. Milk powder is often advertised for the purpose but is an unnecessarily expensive way of getting protein into a mature horse. Most vets and nutritionists advise that mature horses cannot, in any case, digest milk.

Feeding high-fat diets to hard-working endurance horses, eventers, hunters and the like is an effective way of providing them with extra energy, particularly if they are at the limits of their appetites. At one time it was believed that horses were poor digesters of fat but research work has shown that this is not the case.

Expert advice should really be sought from a nutritionist or a vet interested in nutrition on devising a suitable diet. A common way of feeding extra fat or oil to horses used to be to give them boiled linseed but there are other more effective and much more convenient ways of doing this now. A good way is to give a tablespoon of soya or corn oil daily mixed a little into each feed. Up to a cupful can be given, on expert advice.

Bran might be thought of as the obvious vehicle for your mix of linseed, barley and molasses but, as explained shortly, it is not now favoured for feeding horses as it used to be.

Most cereal grains naturally contain some fat, barley containing more than oats, usually. High-fat diets should also be high in choline and vitamin E to ensure adequate chemical breakdown during digestion – consult your vet or nutritionist if in doubt on this.

Fibre is mainly what provides the essential bulk to a horse's diet, so necessary for giving him that comfortable full feeling of satisfaction after a meal. Also referred to as 'roughage', it is the woody part of vegetable matter and is of two types: *cellulose* which is a form of carbohydrate and can be digested, and *lignin* which is indigestible and can be seen as little 'splinters' in a horse's droppings. The purpose of the indigestible lignin is to physically break up the concentrated feed and allow the digestive juices to penetrate and do their job. The intestine is also stimulated by the fibre to work actively and, in fact, cannot do so effectively if there is not enough material passing down it. The importance of adequate bulky fibre/roughage should therefore not be under-estimated. Many people, in my experience, do not feed enough.

Fibre is found in large amounts in straws, hay and hay-age and

forms the outside husk of grains, with oats having considerably
more than barley. Coarse mixes and cubes contain fibre, but even
complete cubes do not contain enough for most horses, who very
quickly become uncomfortably hungry and bored without their hay
to chew on. This results in mental problems and, in some cases,
physical ones, too. If complete cubes are fed, I recommend also
feeding at least half the normal hay diet, preferably mainly at
night.

A far better 'complete' method of feeding horses is available,
based on providing horses with all the nutrients they need in only
one type of roughage or bulk feed, being marketed often as 'forage'
feeds. There are different brands on the market such as the range of
Dengie Feeds (the Hi-Fi and Alfa-A ranges in particular) and
Topflight's Hayplus, Haylite and Haylean. These sorts of feeds aim
to supply different categories of horses and ponies (according to
their nutritional requirements) with well-balanced feeds of the
correct energy grades for them in a form which provides plenty of
bulk with a higher nutrient content than hay or many hayages but
in a far more easily digested form than conventional concentrates
which are, particularly in large amounts, difficult for the horse to
digest and an unnatural feed for the horse's digestive system.

Fortunately, due to the research going on in the field of equine
nutrition, we can expect many more improved feeds of this nature
to come on to the market. They will ultimately result in more
correctly- and appropriately-fed horses, contented and well-
nourished, with the benefit of their being able to eat much more
naturally and almost continuously and still be made hard and fit
for strenuous work, for growth, for breeding or whatever. From
the owner's point of view, this method of feeding is simpler,
quicker and surer and it is particularly appropriate for working
owners who are away from their horses for long periods of time
daily as the horses can be left with sufficient feed of a consistent
and adequate nutritional content to keep them occupied during
long hours in the stable or in a yard or paddock, depending on
grazing facilities and the time of year.

The best way to keep an outdoor horse warm from the point of
view of feeding is *not* to pump spaced-out concentrate feeds into
him as the boost these provide is soon over, but to give him
nutritious roughage such as top quality hay, hayage or a forage
feed. Eating uses up energy (although obviously not as much as it
creates if the food is good) and the use of energy creates heat in the

body, providing the horse with a constantly boosted personal central heating system. The new forage feeds, at any time of year, are a boon to horses and working owners alike.

Vitamins, minerals and trace elements are the content of those expensive and confusing supplements we see on the shelves of saddlers, feed merchants and in the pages of every horsy journal going. Vitamins, minerals and trace elements are essential in the diet, being necessary for the processing of the other feed constituents and certain body functions, the full explanation of which is outside the scope of this book.

It is tempting, when we see a lavishly advertised product, to rush out and buy it, believing that it will give our horse a new zest for life and enable him to win Badminton with no other help, but in practice indiscriminate feeding of these supplements is not only expensive but can cause 'overdosing' and imbalances. Many good makes of cubes and coarse mixes are fully supplemented anyway, but there is always the problem of knowing just what is in the hay/hay-age we are feeding. Good brands of hayage will surely have an analysis panel on the bag which will help your vet or nutritionist integrate the product into the horse's entire dict, and hay can be analysed to get the same information although the best merchants should be able to provide this information anyway. As mentioned, I do feel it is worth the relatively economical fee of an expert to get reliable advice on what components, if any, should be supplemented, and whether a broad-spectrum (wide-ranging) product or simply a single, specialist one – maybe even a single vitamin or mineral – should be used.

The horse can make certain substances within his body and can convert others and because of this, or because his diet already contains what is needed, supplementation might not be necessary.

Owners who prefer to feed straightforward feeds such as oats, bran, barley, maize and so on rather than professionally made compounds can, unwittingly, be feeding diets which are seriously deficient or unbalanced. In these cases, a supplement might well be needed. Again, advice should be sought as no 'ordinary' (professional or amateur) horse owner or manager has the detailed and, hopefully, up-to-date knowledge of a scientifically qualified expert.

Types of Feed

Plainly, we must ensure that horses are fed correctly according to their individual requirements. Grass-fed horses can, provided the grass is reasonable in quality, perform gentle hacking work without any other food. However, if harder work is required the answer is not to put the horse on richer grazing. Remember that grass is very bulky; apart from rich grazing (particularly nitrogen-rich spring grass) often having serious effects, such as laminitis, colic and azoturia, on horses, the sheer weight of food in the intestine is hardly conducive to strenuous work. The horse is unlikely to limit his intake himself, so we must do it for him by restricting his time at grass.

In fact, of course, working horses are fed concentrated foods by us to provide nourishment without bulk. We are all familiar with the hay (grass without all that heavy, bulky water), oats, barley, cubes, coarse mixes, etc. that we commonly feed working horses (and, of course, those on poor grazing, particularly in cold weather when extra food is essential to keep condition on the horse and help him maintain his body temperature). By using such foods, we can give the horse the fuel he needs without weighing him down with the fibrous bulk and water present in grass. It would be impossible for the horse to eat enough grass to provide the nourishment for hard work without also overloading himself with bulk and weight, two factors which go together when grass is eaten. A grass seed mix specially formulated for athletic working horses will go a long way towards greatly reducing these problems as the resulting nutrient content is more suited to them.

A working horse has enough to do to carry or pull us around without being burdened with his own excess body weight, so we help him perform our work by giving him more suitable food.

Having accepted that the horse's digestive system needs small amounts of food constantly passing along it, we have to consider what foods to use to keep him feeling physically comfortable, to provide his nutritional needs without weighing him down with unnecessary bulk, and so to keep him in a fit condition to perform the work we ask of him.

Hay is the most important 'foundation' food for horses. Their digestive system, as we have seen, cannot work effectively without a certain amount of bulky roughage to give a feeling of satisfaction and fullness, to stimulate the movements of the digestive tract and to mix in with the concentrates to break them up and enable the digestive juices to penetrate and do their job. Hay, of course, is grass, cut and dried out of most of its moisture and preserved for long term use.

A slightly different form of roughage feed (which, like good hay, contains in addition to the roughage enough nourishment to keep the horse going nicely for light to medium work depending on analysis or simply maintenance of life) is hay-age; sometimes called haylage. This type of product contains more moisture than hay and is, in effect, a cross between hay and silage. (Silage is wet cut grass which is 'pickled' in its own juices to preserve it and is used extensively to feed cattle in winter. The Irish National Stud ran successful trials during the 1970s using silage to feed horses and ponies, but for the average 'small' horse owner it is not really practical as it is very messy, difficult to handle and is best fed from a self-feed or free-feed clamp or other container from which the horses simply help themselves.)

Hay-age is commercially produced for horse owners and comes vacuum packed in tough polythene sacks, enabling it to be stored outdoors and releasing valuable covered facilities for other things such as stabling or shelter. The polythene sacks can usefully be used, especially in residential areas, for putting droppings and/or used bedding into for sale, thus doing away with the need for the muck heap which often causes complaints from neighbours.

Hay and hay-age are classed as bulk or roughage foods, and good samples are quite adequate for even moderately hard work. Being moist, hay-age is particularly good for horses with respiratory problems who are allergic to the spores often found on even an apparently good, clean sample of hay and which often cause the condition commonly known as 'broken wind' – correctly, chronic obstructive pulmonary disease (C.O.P.D.). It is, however, suitable for all horses. Like any new food, it should be introduced slowly by being mixed at first with the normal hay ration and the proportion gradually increased until hay-age has replaced all the hay. A complaint about feeding haylage in the past has been that you have to feed less than with hay as it is more nutritious and that horses get through their ration quicker so are left without food and occupation. These problems can be overcome by using a lower-energy grade of hayage so you can feed more and by giving it in one of the special small-mesh haynets which force horses to fiddle out only small amounts at a time and so take longer over eating.

Apart from being valuable foods, hay and hay-age, because they need considerable chewing, keep horses occupied during long idle hours and are their equivalent of reading books or watching television! They can give a horse many hours of contented munching, after which he will probably lie down and rest if given a suitable area, and an ad lib supply of such food is an invaluable aid to working horse owners.

It is never a good idea to work a horse immediately after a feed because of the digestive and respiratory problems this can cause. The stomach and lungs lie right next to one another, separated only by a strong but thin sheet of muscle called the diaphragm between the chest cavity and the abdomen which contains the stomach and intestines. During work, the lungs have to expand and the heart has to work more than during rest. If they are hampered by a neighbouring full stomach their action could be interfered with, as could that of the stomach by the expanding lungs and rapidly beating heart. With ad lib supplies of hay/hay-age, however, horses rarely gorge themselves as do those who are left for long periods without food.

If you arrange matters so that your horse will have finished his hay an hour or two before you intend working him, you will avoid such problems. This is invaluable when you want to exercise him in the early mornings before going to work. If you leave him enough hay to last him until the small hours, you can (knowing he is not particularly hungry) safely take him out without his breakfast and thus without working him straight after a feed or waiting for him to digest one.

You can work out how much hay to leave by first leaving so much that he still has some left in the morning. Weigh what he has left, and deduct the figure from the total amount you left him the night before. For his next night's ration, take the resulting figure (the amount he actually ate) and leave him about 2 kg (4 to 5 lbs) *less* than that. This amount should be enough to leave him satisfied and not wanting to eat his bed, and will mean he is not hungry in the morning yet is not too 'full' to exercise first thing. (Obviously, it is always wise to 'walk the first mile out and the last mile home', as the old adage goes.)

In the morning, exercise the horse first, then give him some hay to nibble on for a short time while you put his tack away, etc. On return, give him his concentrate feed, if appropriate, and finally leave him with a full supply of hay to eat and digest in peace while you go off to earn the money to buy him some more! Alternatively, you could give him his concentrate feed, stock up his shelter with hay while he is eating it and then turn him into the paddock or yard to eat his hay ration while you are at work. These practices save you a good deal of time and, as mentioned, avoid working the horse on a full stomach or waiting for his breakfast to go down.

Another version of roughage feed is 'chop' (sometimes called 'chaff'), which is hay and/or hay-age and/or straw chopped up into small pieces about 2 cm (1 in) long. This can usefully be mixed with the concentrate feed and, apart from forcing the horse to chew his food steadily and thoroughly, it aids digestion in the same way as hay. If using the method described above of feeding the horse his concentrates on return from exercise, it is a good idea to add some chop to the feed to provide this aid to digestion and to prevent the horse from gobbling his feed down if he has become hungry. Chop can either be bought from feed merchants or you can get a small chop cutting machine from most good stable suppliers and do your own at home. It doesn't take much time and is well worthwhile. There are various brands of molassed chop on the market which most horses love (and the molasses content will not make a significant difference to the energy content of his diet).

In years when hay is poor or hard to get, some owners – notably racehorse trainers and the like – pay vast sums of money for imported hay or simply to snaffle up whatever good hay *is* around. This is quite unnecessary and a false economy. Hay-age, or even good oat straw – cattle-fodder straw which contains grasses or barley straw which has had the prickly awns removed during harvesting – may well be cheaper. As such feeds are lower in food value than good hay or hay-age, the shortfall will have to be made up with extra concentrates (consult your vet or nutritionist), but this is still cheaper than paying outrageous prices for hay.

With all such feeds as hay, hay-age or feed-straws, it is always cheaper to buy a crop 'off the field' while it is still growing if you can, provided you stipulate that the purchase depends on the resulting quality being good. Buying at harvest time, or at least as early in the autumn as you can, is also a good idea. The price will invariably go up as winter passes and you could be paying double the autumn price by spring or certainly by early summer. In fact, it normally works out cheaper to pay rent on storage space and buy a big load – often even getting an overdraft from the bank and paying interest on it – than to suffer high fodder prices in the early half of the year.

The forage feeds mentioned go a long way towards solving your hay problems as they are bulky by nature yet nutritious in themselves.

Bran is another type of bulk feed which is simply a processed form of the outer, fibrous husk of wheat grains. Bran has for generations been a valued feed for horses, used to pad out a concentrate feed and to make the ubiquitous bran mash which we have been told by our predecessors is a valuable easily digested feed for a tired or sick horse and which is commonly described as a laxative feed.

In fact, bran can be dispensed with quite easily. Its use for adding bulk to concentrate feed is better met by chop. Its use for making bran mashes is quite unnecessary. If the horse needs a laxative, there is probably something more wrong with the entire diet, feeding regime and digestion than can be put right by a bran mash. If a mash is fed because the horse is on a day off, 'false' feeds of chop, diluted molasses, molassine meal, soaked sugar-beet pulp, grass meal and/or thinly sliced roots such as carrots are more appropriate.

Hydroponically-grown grass (grown using water and possibly liquid nutrients but no soil) is also an excellent and nutritious succulent to feed and 'home' units are becoming more and more affordable for small yards.

Bran mashes are *not* easily digested feeds suitable for tired or sick horses. Bran is, in truth, not easy to digest but hard, which is why it has a laxative effect on the gut: a natural reaction is to get rid of something which cannot be processed as quickly as possible. The last thing a tired or sick horse needs is a feed which is difficult to digest; far better give him coarsely grated carrots, soaked sugar beet pulp, cut grass (although not fine lawn clippings which can ferment and cause serious colic) and add a single handful of his normal concentrate feed to keep the digestive bacteria going.

Bran mashes are also unappetising (as confirmed by the advice to add a handful of salt or oats to make it more acceptable!) so again they are not the sort of feed you would want to give a horse who needs his appetite stimulating.

A final point against the use of bran from a health point of view is that it can create an imbalance in the diet between phosphorous and calcium. Bran is rich in phosphorous itself and contains a substance which blocks the absorption of calcium from other foods. The resulting excess of phosphorous can cause brittle, porous and enlarged bones prone to fracture and other problems.

If it is felt that a little bran improves the texture of the feed or provides a useful base for mixing in medicine, make sure it *is* a little – no more than one part bran to six of concentrates (by weight, not volume).

From the point of view of economy, bran is undoubtedly an expensive feed. Good bran (broad flakes and plenty of flour) is now very hard to get and even more expensive than the poorer sort resembling sawdust. I have to admit I often feel feed merchants play on this and on the fact that most horse owners feel they cannot live without it, never mind their horses. So save money and don't bother too much about using bran.

If your horse has to be off work and largely stabled for some time, perhaps due to injury or illness, ask the makers of your usual cube or coarse mix if they make an 'invalid' feed. Some do, and these provide all essential nutrients without overfeeding. In conjunction with hay and roots, for essential succulence, they can prove ideal feeds for horses in such conditions.

Roots are usually loved by horses and the favourites seem to be carrots. A few horses will eat turnips and swedes and many love fodder beets (which contain a good deal of carbohydrate). The latter three can be left in a horse's manger for him to crunch on during the night or a long day.

Roots can be too expensive to buy from a greengrocer even if you only have one horse, but you could get a supply of stockfeed carrots (or whatever root your horse prefers) from an agricultural merchant. These are simply misshapen items unattractive to the domestic consumer and are much cheaper than the more commercial sort. If not fed whole, as large items like turnips can be, they should not be fed in chunks but coarsely grated or thinly sliced: if fed in chunks the horse could get one stuck in his oesophagus. Called 'choke', this is not actually choke as we think of it (i.e. something stuck and blocking the windpipe) but it can be extremely unpleasant for the horse and can have serious consequences. It always calls for the services of a vet, and all food and water should be withheld till he or she arrives. (The horse will show 'choke' by having obvious difficulty in swallowing. Sometimes the lump can be seen in the oesophagus in the lower part of the neck and, if he has continued to eat, food or water and saliva may start coming down one or both nostrils.)

Sugar beet pulp has been a popular root for horses for years now and, particularly the molassed sort, is liked by most. It is available in loose flakes or compressed into cubes. Although trials have taken place which appeared to show that horses can, in fact, consume large quantities of dry pulp without harm, it is not something I would risk or recommend. I stick to the advice always given of thoroughly soaking the pulp, particularly the cubes, in at least six times its own volume of cold water, and for a good twenty-four hours before feeding. It is not advisable to soak it in hot water as it can quickly ferment and cause digestive problems. It also has the advantage of being high in calcium so can balance a typical old-fashioned high phosphorus diet comprising grain (oats, barley) and bran, so if you know anyone who simply cannot adjust their attitude and continues to feed in this way try to encourage them to feed plenty of soaked sugar beet pulp!

Concentrate feeds are so called because they contain comparatively little fibrous roughage compared with hay and hay-age. Those most commonly used for horses in Europe and North America (and in other countries, too) are oats (for generations a traditional food for horses) and barley. Some cooked, flaked maize (corn) is used, and in America this forms the staple concentrate ration of very many horses, particularly in the western and southern states. Maize is high in energy and low in protein and fibre so you must counterbalance this characteristic with other ingredients to maintain a balanced diet.

Wheat and rye are not normally used, more because of cost (they are principal human feeds) than unsuitability. Like any grain, if they are introduced very gradually into the diet they are quite suitable, if expensive.

Oats are very palatable to horses. They are best fed freshly rolled or crushed to crack the outer husk. If they have been crushed for over a week, there is a possibility that they are starting to go 'off' to the extent that they are not fit to feed. Many top-class yards crush their own oats daily, buying bulk supplies of whole grain and storing them in hoppers. This is not feasible for many owners but, if it can be arranged, it is a good plan to go and buy your oats whole and then ask the merchant to crush them while you wait! The grains should be plump with plenty of body, not long and thin when they will be nearly all husk.

Whole oats have a habit of passing through the horse unchewed as many horses simply do not bother to crush them up properly with their teeth. As the outer husk is largely indigestible fibre, the digestive juices cannot get into the nutritious part of the grain and it is completely wasted.

Oats do have a rather intoxicating so-called 'heating' effect on some horses, particularly cobs and ponies, and some actually seem to be allergic to them, coming out in spots and developing itchy, flaky skin. Some animals become really silly when fed oats and are dangerous if under-exercised. If a horse or pony is used for novice or moderate riders, it is probably better to use some other concentrate instead.

Oats do give extra zest to sluggish or hardworking animals and, because of their popularity and their traditional status, they will remain in use for many years yet, price permitting. It should be noted that they are deficient in an important protein constituent, lysine, so advice should be taken with regard to supplementing.

Barley as a 'straight' feed is a very practical one for a horse who either cannot take oats or whose exercise is restricted due to his or his owner's circumstances. It should be fed rolled (not crushed to a pulp when it loses much nutriment) just so as to crack this very hard grain. Cooked, flaked barley is also available. Boiled barley has long been an 'invalid' feed or one used to put weight on thin horses, although the amounts usually fed wouldn't make that much difference in practice to most horses. Cooking feeds is unnecessary nowadays due to the improved nutrient content and digestibility of modern branded feeds.

However, as many horses love boiled barley for a treat (as with linseed), it is as well to know how to make it. Simply place the required amount of grains in a large sieve (for one horse) and lay the sieve over a large pan of boiling water on the cooker. The steam rises through the grains and cooks and softens them. Stir the grains over regularly until they are all thoroughly soft, and then mix them with the feed. As far more harm can come from slightly overfeeding a horse than slightly underfeeding, the amount of barley used should be deducted from the normal ration.

Horse cubes (or nuts) and coarse mixes are very popular for feeding to horses, and they are convenient. There are many different makes on the market, some of them excellent, and a vet or nutritionist could advise you which would be best for your particular circumstances if you get the analyses.

Cubes contain many different ingredients bound together, usually in a molassed base to form pellets, whereas coarse mixes are simply those different ingredients mixed loosely together. A good product will be properly balanced as regards protein, carbohydrates, fats, minerals and vitamins, and you will probably get better results than feeding straights (i.e. separate ingredients such as oats or barley with bran) and perhaps an expensive supplement which takes your fancy because of an eye-catching advertisement in a horse magazine! The supplement itself may well be a superb product, but not right for your particular horse. With cubes and coarse mixes, you simply have to weigh out the correct amount, and you should then have no problems about dietary balance.

A commonly given reason for not using cubes is: 'I like to see what I'm feeding.' Actually, although with such feeds as oats and barley, you know that they are oats and barley, you still cannot 'see' what you are feeding because unless you have them analysed you do not know exactly what is in them. With cubes and coarse mixes at least the analysis is on the bag – and I have yet to come across a sack of oats with that information on it.

This does not mean that I am against feeding oats and barley – far from it – but I am against feeding an ingredient of unknown content. I therefore feel it advisable, whatever ingredients you want to feed, to enlist the professional help of a veterinary surgeon or an equine nutritionist/management consultant in getting your horse's diet formulated and the ingredients (including the hay) analysed. It will be more economical in the long run and more effective from your horse's point of view.

It may be that the ingredients you want to use, or can obtain, make up into a diet deficient in some nutrient or other and that a supplement is needed to balance it. Advice should be sought as to the best type. There are many supplements on the market now, most of them very expensive. Some are broad spectrum (containing a wide range of different vitamins and minerals) and others are specialised (containing only one or two) and it is important to use the correct one, not only for the health of your horse but for the health of your bank balance, too.

The Importance of Consistency

We are constantly told never to make sudden changes in feeding but it is not usually stressed that this applies to every single feed, not merely to the diet as a whole. Because of the sensitive nature of the horse's digestive system and the fact that, in nature, he eats a little of the same ingredients all the time, we should mimic this and feed the same ingredients in *every feed* varying only the *amounts* given. For instance, if your horse is suddenly thrown out of work your instinct should be to drastically cut down, or cut out, his concentrates particularly if he is to be box-bound. Proceed by cutting concentrates by half, then half again and so on till he is getting no more than a single handful in each feed, making up the amount by increasing the quantities in each feed of other ingredients such as chop, sugar beet pulp, maybe some grass meal, grated carrots and so on.

The point is that whatever ingredients you use must be those he is already used to, so always use *some* of each ingredient in his diet in each feed. The reason for this is that the horse largely digests his food by means of microscopic bacteria and protozoa in his intestines. These micro-organisms, as they are known, actually digest the horse's food for him, using it as their own food, and they, too, need a consistent, reliable diet! If they don't get it they die off and are not available when more of 'their' type of food comes along, at least not in sufficient numbers to do a good job, so the horse suffers either incomplete digestion, indigestion or actual colic. Apart from being bad management this is also wasteful. The micro-organisms are known to start dying off in as little as four hours if they are starved due to an inconsistent diet passing down the digestive tract.

For this reason, also, new ingredients must be introduced very gradually so that the population of appropriate micro-organisms has a chance to build up to sufficient numbers to digest it.

Do not, therefore, feed, for example, cubes for breakfast, coarse mix for lunch, straights for tea and so on. Do not feed a weekly bran mash for the same reason (among others already mentioned). Do not change from one batch of the same food to another but gradually mix a little of the new batch with the old till you eventually change over. This applies to each fresh batch of hay, hayage, forage, cubes, coarse mix, chop or straights. It is easy to arrange once you get used to operating on this principle, and it is so important to your horse's digestive system and wellbeing.

Judging Quality

From a practical point of view, there are certain steps you can take to ensure that the feed you are offered is of reasonable quality, although this in itself will not confirm its actual feeding value.

Firstly, any food which smells unpleasant in that it seems sour, musty or dirty should be turned down. Good hay, in particular, is usually noted for its 'nose' or pleasant, sweet aroma. Taste grains such as oats: they should be sweet and starchy-tasting. Cubes usually taste horrible to us but a guide to their quality is smell and appearance. There should be no sour smell and they should be hard and dry. If soft and damp, refuse them. Coarse mixes, like grain, should smell sweet or of nothing in particular. Some do appear moist because of additives like molasses. Molassine meal goes off very quickly in warm weather so it is normally better not to use it then, but to buy black treacle in tins. The same goes for molassed sugar-beet pulp – in warm weather I find it best to use the un-molassed type and add treacle separately.

Feeds containing molasses or some kind of damping or binding syrup as is the case with many coarse mixes soon go 'off' in warm weather. It is therefore a good idea to buy a large second-hand fridge (not a freezer), remove the shelves and store sacks of such feed in there to keep it in usable condition, otherwise it could make your horse ill (if he eats it at all) or simply end up having to be thrown on the muck heap.

As a working owner, you might find it difficult to arrange deliveries. Usually someone has to sign for a consignment, and they usually arrive while you are at work. This could mean that you have to call for your own feed, inconvenient though this is. You may be able to make arrangements with someone else to accept your delivery, but unfortunately this means you cannot check the quality of your shipment before signing, which is highly desirable – particularly in the case of a firm you have never dealt with before.

Some of the less reputable merchants keep their best fodder for farmers and big owners, palming off the sub-standard stuff on to horse owners who they think don't know any better and will pay through the nose for almost anything. Learn to judge quality, therefore; ask questions about analysis and religiously send or take back any feed which is no good. When you are able to be present for your own deliveries, undo the sacks (except possibly those containing branded cubes or coarse mixes) and check the quality *before* signing.

Remember that hay-age usually comes in vacuum-compressed polythene sacks. If these are punctured and air gets in, the quality of the contents can be very seriously affected and so, therefore, can your horse's health. If you open a sack and there is a suspicion of a sour smell, don't use any of it at all and ring the merchant at once. Do not be reassured that it is alright, but explain that it is actually sour and acrid and is unfit to feed. You are protected by your rights as a consumer, and anything you buy must be of 'merchantable quality' – in other words, fit for the purpose for which you bought it. This is a powerful lever on your behalf.

In appearance, hay should be greenish to golden, with closed seed heads. If the seed heads are open, it has obviously 'gone to seed' and its feeding value will be much lower than it would otherwise be. If the hay is dull, stemmy rather than leafy, brassy or washy yellow or brownish and smells either musty or sour – maybe even with visible white or black mould on it and giving off clouds of dust when shaken out – it is not even fit for bedding, although you could perhaps use it (after receiving a very substantial discount from the supplier) for stacking up and making a three-sided shelter within a sturdy wooden framework and adding a rigid corrugated polythene roof. This is all such hay is fit for.

When you open a bale of hay it should spring apart rather than stay where it is or simply drop lifelessly apart, and the hay should be easy to shake out (with no sign of dust); it should feel and look glossy and smooth and have a sweet, appetising smell. Hay which smells like tobacco is often thought to be good but in fact it is slightly mowburnt (in other words, it overheated in the rick during 'making') and will not be of particularly good feeding value. It may even be harmful, although many horses love it just as many humans love cigarettes!

Research work in Scotland has shown that samples of hay given to expert horsemasters for quality judging were rated according to traditional methods and opinions. When each sample was compared with the actual laboratory analysis, it turned out that the most desirable samples from the horsemasters' points of view often had poor feeding value compared with other samples they had down-rated. So judging hay in this traditional manner should, perhaps, be regarded as no more than a general guide to what *not* to buy – that is, buy nothing dirty, mouldy, dusty or sour/musty smelling. Anything else, get analysed so as to be sure what you are feeding. Really good merchants may well have an analysis all ready for you, if they are conscientious.

Straw, whether intended for feeding or bedding, should be subject to the same sight-and-smell tests. Mouldy straw is every bit as dangerous to a horse's health due to spores inhaled or ingested, whether by accident or by design. If you intend to feed the straw, get it analysed so you can get the rest of the diet balanced.

Compounds versus Straights

Although compound feeds (cubes and coarse mixes) are, when of a reliable brand, properly balanced as regards energy, protein, vitamins etc., many people still find it hard not to tinker with their horses' diets and add a bit of this and a bit of that in the form of other ingredients which have a significant feeding value and which do, inevitably, throw the diet out of balance. You can add things like roots, molasses, honey and so on if you wish but *not* other staple feeds like oats, barley, flaked maize *or* mix brands of cubes or coarse mixes together as this practice will make a nonsense of the carefully worked out and balanced diet provided by the manufacturers of a good make of cubes or coarse mix. The same goes for adding 'goodies' to the forage feeds which are in themselves balanced. Roots and so on are all right but not other main feeds such as cubes, coarse mixes, straights, bran or whatever. You are doing your horse no favours by doing this and are purposely unbalancing his diet. Feed supplements, too, should not be added to already-balanced feeds without truly expert advice (from a nutritionist or vet), even broad-spectrum (general) ones as they will probably be superfluous and maybe disadvantageous or even dangerous.

Feed products known as protein concentrates and cereal balancers could be useful in balancing a diet composed largely of straw or hay of poor nutritional content or balance. They are compounded feeds intended to be fed with other ingredients, usually cereals (grain feeds such as oats, barley, maize and also bran) but can be used with non-cereal diets such as hay, hayage and straw provided the manufacturers' instructions are followed very carefully or they are fed according to the advice of a competent equine nutritionist. They will inevitably alter the balance of the whole ration which is why expert advice is needed on how to use them with the horse's existing or intended rations. If, for example, you are feeding oat straw and a conventional coarse mix, you could use a balancer to make up for the different feeding value of the straw and still use your coarse mix as well. The nutritionist at the firm whose products you are thinking of using should be able to offer you the correct advice, or a private nutritionist or vet interested in nutrition.

Quantity

The most reliable way to calculate how much feed to give a horse is to use his bodyweight as a guide; this is made quite simple by using one of the special 'tape-measures' designed for the purpose (available from some nutritionists, feed firms and some veterinary practices mentioned earlier). These save a lot of calculating and messing about (no need to trek to the nearest weighbridge or work out from the results how much total food to give). The tapes are graduated so that you simply read off the horse's measurement round the girth, and his weight and consequent daily food requirement.

Alternatively, you can measure round the horse's girth just behind the withers, making sure the binder twine, tape measure or whatever you are using is straight and that you take the measurement at the end of one of the horse's *out* breaths. Then, using the following tables, you can read off the horse or pony's total daily food requirement

Ponies

Girth in inches	40	42.5	45	47.5	50	52.5	55	57.5
Girth in cm	101	108	114	120	127	133	140	146
Bodyweight in lb	100	172	235	296	368	430	502	562
Bodyweight in kg	45	77	104	132	164	192	234	252

Horses

Girth in inches	55	57.5	60	62.5	65	67.5
Girth in cm	140	146	152	159	165	171
Bodyweight in lb	538	613	688	776	851	926
Bodyweight in kg	240	274	307	346	380	414

Girth in inches	70	72.5	75	77.5	80	82.5
Girth in cm	178	184	190	199	203	206
Bodyweight in lb	1014	1090	1165	1278	1328	1369
Bodyweight in kg	453	486	520	570	593	611

(Tables based on work of Glushanok, Rochlitz and Skay, 1981)

Horses and some ponies and cobs will usually need 2 kg per 100 kg bodyweight (2 lb per 100 lb). Ponies and cobs who easily get fat should receive less, particularly concentrates. It is more accurate, of course, to weigh your animal on a weighbridge but if you haven't access to one the above method will be found to be a very good substitute.

Just about any animal should be fed so that you cannot actually see its ribs but can feel them quite easily, so once you have the above starting point you can easily adjust the diet accordingly to keep it in good condition, neither too fat nor too thin. Physical fitness usually means getting rid of excess fat and building up muscle in its place. Those animals doing hard work and which are naturally lean may just show the last two pairs of ribs but there is no excuse for any more showing. The horse's type as well as his individual tendencies should also be considered. For example a 15 hands high cob may look fat to the naked eye compared with a 15 hands high Arab but both may be in good condition for their types and work.

How to split the total ration between concentrates and roughage for horses on a conventional diet (as opposed to one of the forage regimes) depends on the work being done. For a horse doing about two hours a day moderately active hacking (mostly walking and trotting with a bit of cantering and jumping), a suggested split is two-thirds (by weight) roughage and one-third concentrates. If you give the horse ad lib hay, you will probably find that he splits it this way himself. You should know how much hay he is eating and may well find that this amount deducted from the total you have estimated results in the figure remaining being what he seems to need in concentrates. This is what I have found in practice.

It will always be a case of 'the eye of the master making the horse fat'; some horses are much better doers than others, requiring less food to keep in good condition than the naturally leaner sort who may never look as rounded as their colleagues yet may be perfectly alright in their own way.

Energy Requirements

What 'grade' of feed to give can also create problems. In the past we have tended to gauge food on its protein content. Racehorse cubes, for instance, were invariably around 14% protein, horse and pony or hunter cubes 11 or 12%. It is more accurate nowadays to go by the energy content of the product. We know that horses need less protein, in general, than was previously believed. Basically, for horses in hard to moderate work, look for products which say on their analysis panels or labels that they contain 10 – 12 MJ (megajoules) of DE (digestible energy) per kilogramme. For animals in light work and for cobs and ponies, 8.5 – 10 MJ DE per kilogramme is enough. Megajoules are simply measurement units of energy (just as centimetres or inches measure length); the term 'digestible energy' is used because not all the energy content of the food your horse eats can be used by his body, and you need to know what amount of energy in a particular food is actually digestible.

All reputable makes of branded feeds give a good analysis table on the bag, whether cubes, coarse mixes, hayage or forage, so you should have no trouble getting this information. Straights such as oats, barley, maize, hay and feeding straws will not have this information unless you are buying from a top-class merchant who has obtained an analysis but you can get samples analysed yourself in a laboratory through your vet or a nutritionist to help you work out the whole diet. You do need to know the energy content and nutritional balance of the entire diet if you are to feed accurately, both concentrates and roughages.

Of course, it is possible to work without this information using the horse's condition as a guide but it can never be so accurate and may result in your feeding, for example, too little of a feed which is too high in energy because the horse is jumping all over the place or going down with laminitis, and ending up with the horse hungry, uncomfortable and prone to wood-chewing and other vices because of this. It is obviously much kinder to the horse and much more effective management to feed enough of a lower-energy grade of feed to keep the horse's appetite satisfied without pumping him over-full of dangerous energy.

This is where branded feeds, concentrates, roughages or forages, come into their own. Not only are they correctly balanced as regards vitamins, minerals, trace elements, fats and proteins but you know for certain what the energy level is so can start out accurately from the beginning instead of having to operate a wait-and-see policy. The diet may need adjusting anyway but any adjustments will be far smaller if you start out with certain knowledge of what you are feeding rather than guessing what

conventional feeds contain – or waiting for the horse to tell you by
his behaviour and condition.

Grass

It is obviously not possible to control a horse's diet absolutely

Fig. 24 Hydroponically-grown grass (requiring no soil) is gradually becoming
more common and provides a quick method of obtaining green feed all year
round, to the benefit of the horses and ponies concerned. Users maintain
savings in feed costs and many claim improved appearance and health in
their animals. This system, suitable for a larger yard, is the 'Hydrograss'
system marketed by Equitus Ltd, Burnt Ash House, Cirencester Road,
Chalford, Stroud, Gloucestershire.

minutely when he is on grass, but in practice this really is not necessary. And I think one has to be realistic in such matters and not develop a fetish about feeding. To keep a horse away from grass, his natural food, simply because one does not know the exact analysis of every mouthful would plainly be quite ridiculous.

Research into equine nutrition continues and we can now feed more and more accurate diets. It is known that grass does contain many nutrients, and herbs do so in particular, which a horse may well not get in an artificial diet except by the possible inclusion of expensive feed supplements. For athletic, working horses, too, hydroponic grass can be given which is sown from seed mixes specially intended for such animals as opposed to, for example, breeding stock or dairy cattle. Low-energy mixes can also be used for animals prone to fat such as good doers, ponies and cobs.

Grass is one of the cheapest feeds you can give your horse. During spring, summer and autumn, it can provide a valuable and much appreciated element in his diet. If the grass is reasonably well cared for and the horse doing little or no work (he could easily do an hour or two's light hacking on grass alone), it could well form all or most of his diet.

Sadly, most horse paddocks are dreadfully neglected; they are overgrazed and littered with droppings. The grass in the lavatory areas (horses designate such areas in their paddocks) grows long and rank for the horses will not graze there, while the grazing areas can become as bald as a billiard table.

To be productive, land and grass do need a little care. For a start, any field expected to produce a reasonable grass crop must be well drained. Wet land is cold and oxygen starved and normally seethes with flies in summer. Soil type varies widely, not only in different parts of the country but from field to field in some localities. Again, expert analysis by a management consultant or fertiliser firm (or through the Equine Services Department of the Agricultural Development Advisory Service section of the Ministry of Agriculture, Fisheries and Foods – see your local telephone book) can let you know what kind of state your land is in, and fertiliser and seed firms usually analyse free if you buy their products.

Weed control can be difficult and a major job on a badly infested field; but room must be made for grass to grow, so useless and harmful vegetation must be removed, in the interests of economy and health. The advice you are given may be to spray or hand pull, as appropriate. Seed mixtures will vary depending on the soil and climate in your area, but it is worthwhile stressing to whoever is helping you that the field is for horses, not cattle. Nitrogen rich varieties (and nitrogen fertilisers producing a quick flush of rich grass) are not suitable for horses and can cause digestive and circulatory troubles. For these reasons, it is as well to consult a specialist equine consultant rather than a farm/cattle-orientated person who may not understand horses' needs. The Equine Services Department of ADAS should be *au fait* with such requirements but it is as well to stress them to whoever you deal with there. Don't be fobbed off by anybody who may not seem to wish to go to the trouble of sorting out a special seed mix for you but wishes to take the easy route of giving you a general mix!

When the vegetation is sorted out, a rota will have to be devised to keep the land in good heart. If you can possibly manage it, divide your land into at least two parts – and preferably three or more – so each can be used, treated and rested in turn. After horses have grazed the land for three or four weeks (not months, as is often the case), you may notice it is taking on a patchy appearance, some areas remaining long and others short. That is the time to move the horses on to the next area and to cut the long grass down and harrow the field to aerate it and pull out dead grass and roots. Apply any fertiliser recommended and finally rest. Continue this rota with the other division(s). It is no longer recommended to scatter droppings even within the lavatory areas as this has been found to spread the eggs and resultant larvae rather than exposing them to the sun and air to be desiccated.

Information is beginning to emerge which suggests that it might not be so beneficial as has been believed up to now to graze horse pastures with cattle. The cattle do eat off the long grass in the horses' lavatory areas (these do not offend the cattle) and drop their own much-needed manure on the horses' grazing areas (which in turn does not bother the horses). Horse parasites taken in by the cattle will die off in an unnatural host and vice versa, but it seems that there are some parasites which are common to both species and that cattle can, therefore, actually infect a paddock with parasites not previously there which can infect the horses in turn.

Your veterinary surgeon or consultant should be able to keep you up to date on these matters and may be able to recommend a suitable anthelmintic (worm medicine) to cater for all needs. It is known that cattle manure does disguise the smell of horse droppings on paddocks and so brings back into use areas which horses may previously have been avoiding. Spreading cattle manure thickly in the autumn would seem to be a good idea for this reason alone (provided the parasite problem can be sorted out), apart from the valuable organic fertiliser it affords. Old-fashioned farmyard manure comprising droppings, urine and straw is now very difficult to obtain in most areas, however, due to the modern tendency to keep the unfortunate animals with no bedding. The resultant slurry is far too rich and lacking in humus to be safe to put on horse paddocks unless you are taking a hay crop first before grazing the horses on the new grass as it is too high in nitrogen.

Picking up the droppings from paddocks if you can possibly manage it can add to the size and value of your manure heap, of course. It can also reduce the risk of worm infection if the task is done daily, particularly on small or overcrowded fields – one horse per half-hectare (one horse per acre), if out round the clock, is regarded as quite enough for a stocking level, and this only if the field is in use for *part* of the year. However, if the horses are wormed regularly every six weeks throughout the year, the numbers of eggs and larvae dropped on the land will be negligible.

The drug ivermectin (marketed as Eqvalan in the UK and Zimecterin in the USA) removes immature, larval forms of redworm in the arterial stages (during the part of their life cycle when they are still circulating in the blood vessels) and because of this has a much greater 'kill' than other drugs as the larvae are killed or severely incapacitated before they reach the intestines to continue maturing and breeding and damaging the horse's intestines. Therefore, it is possible to worm with invermectin less often than with wormers which do not kill arterial stages of worms. However, although it kills intestinal worms (including redworms, the most dangerous) and bots, and also lungworms, it does not kill tapeworm which is becoming more significant in horse popula-tions. The drug pyrantel does kill these, however, plus redworms and others, but not bots.

To keep the infestation of your paddocks and horses down to a minimum and to be sure you are worming your horse frequently enough with the right drugs for the worms he has, you must consult your veterinary surgeon who can carry out various tests on the horses' droppings and perhaps do blood tests, too, to find out what worms are present and to work out an effective programme for your circumstances. Sometimes the drug may need changing, sometimes the dose level and timing can also be important. For instance, to kill bots you need to worm with a boticide (a drug which kills bots) after the first frost of the autumn or winter. The frost will kill the adult females which lay the eggs and the subsequent worming will kill their immature bots inside your horses. If everyone in the country did this just once bots would become extinct in the UK! (Unless they flew over from elsewhere in the spring.)

If you are in the unfortunate but common situation of keeping your horse at an establishment where the other owners will not agree to join in a proper worming programme and all worm at the same time, you can at least keep your own horse's infestation levels down reasonably by using ivermectin most of the time to remove immature and mature parasites, with pyrantel occasionally to deal with tapeworms, as required, according to your vet's advice.

As mentioned previously, *all* horses and ponies using the field must be wormed at the same time – and every time – if infection is to be avoided. This goes for any donkeys, too. With the latter there is still the risk of lungworm being passed on, so discuss matters with your vet if this is your situation.

It is, of course, very difficult to care properly for land which is not your own or which you only have casual use of and are not 'The Boss'. If you keep your horse at a communal do-it-yourself yard, with or without a caring manager/proprietor on hand, it is well worthwhile getting all the other owners together and making sure they all realise the advantages of removing droppings from the field and, even more important, of having all the horses wormed at the same time.

If you have the use of the land for a reasonable period, say several months, a year or more, whether the land is your own or not, you will find that a little time and money spent on getting it into shape will pay dividends in an improved grass crop for the nutrition and pleasure of your animals. Those on suitable pasture with enough to eat rarely get into trouble by trying to jump out in search of greener pastures, by experimenting with poisonous plants or by stirring up a fracas among the other horses because they are bored or hungry. It really is cheaper to buy fertiliser to improve grass than to buy extra feed – and even the hardest working and fittest horses (including racehorses) benefit from time spent at grass, even an hour or so providing a welcome mental and physical break from the usual work/stable/hard feed routine.

Getting the work done may not be easy, but the regular jobs can be done by family/friends/other 'commune' owners. Such tasks as cutting the long grass can be done by battery or motor-powered lawnmowers (if you use the kind with a grass box, scatter the grass on the over-grazed areas to rot down there and add valuable nutrients) or even by scythe if you can get hold of one these days – they are not that difficult to use once you get the knack. Ideally an agricultural gang mower would be best as it makes light work of the job.

Droppings can be picked up by hand on a rota basis, fertiliser can be spread from the back of a truck, horse-drawn trailer, van, Land Rover or hatchback car on a still day, and a sensible horse can easily be rigged up cheaply and taught to pull a chain harrow over the field. Probably the only contract labour you will have to pay for is muck spreading and any drainage operations, of course.

As regards getting cattle to graze on your land, there is no reason why you cannot be as canny as (in my experience) most farmers are and get them to pay for your grass. Offer them cut-price rates (judge it by perusing adverts for grazing in the local farming press) and put the money in your kitty budget, which should then be able to pay for the fertiliser, a second-hand chain harrow, etc. Cattle should be polled (hornless) as most are these days, and free from diseases such as ringworm; this last topic should be discussed with your veterinary surgeon who can give you details of what cattle diseases could be dangerous to your horses.

Problems over routine can arise in communal yards; it may be necessary for individual owners to vary their routines so that incompatible grazing companions are not turned out together if injuries are to be avoided. Also, horses in communal yards tend to be brought to and from the paddocks and in and out from exercise at widely varying times according to their owners' schedules. This sometimes worries owners who prefer to feed not only at regular times (usually given as one of the golden rules of feeding) but also at the same time as other horses, to prevent any 'left out' feelings. It is true that, if horses *are* fed all at the same time and at regular hours, they do indeed come to expect it, and can create havoc if their routine is broken or some are left out, making slaves of their owners.

Think what happens, however, to horses regularly taken away to shows, etc. Their routine is invariably broken to some extent and horses in the stable areas are certainly not fed all at the same time. Police horses are another example; these are genuine working animals who have to adapt to work circumstances and requirements. They return to the stables at varying hours throughout the day and night and are fed as and when it is convenient, within reason, although feed is usually taken away in their horseboxes with them. Some horses will be at home and will already have been fed when the latecomers arrive; they do not kick up a fuss when the latter are fed, partly because they are used to this irregular pattern but partly also because they have already had their own feed and are not hungry.

I have found this is the 'secret' of being able to feed horses at different times in the same yard without problems: not letting any of the animals in the yard get really hungry. It also works if, because you work irregular shifts, you cannot arrange identical feed times every day for your horse. Leave him enough hay or other roughage to keep him occupied and prevent hunger and the actual time is not that important within an hour or so: this is one of the advantages of the branded forage feeds as the horse gets pretty well the same thing all the time so digestive upsets cannot occur due to erratic feeding of spaced-out concentrate feeds. Also, leave instructions for someone else to feed him if at all possible.

I have recommended more than once that it is a good idea to have the field shelter stocked up with hay to keep the horses happy and occupied when the grass is not up to much. In communal yards, again, it may not be easy at first try to organise this. There is no point in one owner putting out hay for her horse if it is going to be eaten by all the others whose owners have *not* done so. However, as in the case of worming, an informal meeting can be called to suggest that all owners contribute a certain amount of money or hay/hay-age every week to a 'field hay' stock, the amounts varying according to their horses' appetites. Then hay can safely be put out for all the horses (obviously one more net or rack than there are horses to ensure that there is always a vacant supply for any timid horse). This will not cost any more on top of normal feed costs, for the horses will only eat what they need anyway and will eat that much less at other times, probably spending stabled hours resting more.

As ever, mutual common sense and co-operation can do nothing but good and everyone will benefit, particularly the horses.

Grooming

Grooming is another time-consuming task and one which can be quite hard work to the inexperienced and unfit. It is certainly necessary, not only because it aids good health and condition but also because it is no pleasure to ride or drive a dirty horse. It is also bad for the reputation of horsepeople everywhere for some of their number to be seen out with unkempt animals.

The horse's skin, like that of other animals, is continually shedding dead scales from its outer layer (this forms the dandruff seen in an ungroomed horse's coat). Skin, like everything else, has a limited lifespan and is continually being shed and replaced throughout the year. The skin also gives out natural oils to lubricate itself and the coat hairs and to give some protection against wet weather and, to a much lesser extent, cold.

The skin also contains the hair follicles from which the coat hairs grow. The hairs, too, are being shed constantly throughout the year, although the main times of casting are spring and autumn.

The amount of grooming a horse receives depends not only on how much time his owner has but on how he is kept and what work he is doing. A fit, stabled horse in fairly hard work will probably get roughly an hour's grooming a day. Grooming, particularly correct body brushing, stimulates the skin, and removes dirt, excess grease and dead skin. If you put tack or harness on top of dried sweat or mud it can easily rub a sore place which may mean the horse cannot be worked normally until it has healed. Therefore, even if pushed for time, the saddle/harness/bridle areas should be brushed free of mud and dried sweat before exercise.

The grooming process, when done sympathetically (gently where necessary, on sensitive areas like head and belly, and firmly where appropriate, such as the long strokes used on the neck, trunk and quarters of the horse) does help build a bond between horse and handler. At the same time it enables the handler to spot any skin irregularities, such as lumps, wounds, rashes or unusual casting, or soreness – either visually, by feel or by noticing the horse's behaviour when being groomed. Dirty coats also harbour parasites such as ticks and lice so, done regularly, grooming is a definite aid to the health and comfort of a horse.

However, although it *is* an important task, there may well be days when you simply haven't time to give your stabled horse a thorough grooming. What should be done every day is the sponging of eyes, nostrils, lips, sheath, udder and dock, including the underside of the tail itself which is often forgotten. Certainly the feet must be picked out and shoes checked twice daily.

Horses at grass are not commonly body brushed, anyway, but should get the same basic attention. Run your hands carefully over every inch of the horse, too, to detect any irregularities.

When body brushing (the main part of the full grooming process), many people use much more strength and energy than necessary because they are doing it incorrectly. Especially if you are doing more than one horse, you need to save energy otherwise you may not have enough to do the job effectively. The body brush should be held with a stiff arm slightly bent at the elbow. Then lean your weight on the arm and so against the horse to push the bristles through the coat, rather than pushing the brush using your arm, shoulder and back muscles. You will find this much less tiring and just as effective.

For real speed, however, try a trick I developed some years ago. Get yourself a tough pair of leather chaps and two of the hand-type metal curry combs, i.e. the type with a fabric or leather band across the back for you to slip your hand into, rather than the type with a wooden handle. Using leather thonging or binder twine, fasten these curry combs to the tops of the thighs of the chaps by passing the thread (or whatever you are using) along the grooves between the metal teeth and into holes (preferably punched to avoid tearing the leather) in the chaps, and tie them together firmly inside the chaps. Do this top and bottom with each curry comb so they are firmly fixed.

Now take a body brush in each hand. Work quickly all over the horse giving long firm strokes with alternate hands (as you normally do with only one hand). When you want to clean the brushes, as you should every three strokes or so, simply scrape them down the curry combs on your thighs, both at the same time. So you are brushing and cleaning like this: left, right, left, right, left, right, scrape, scrape; left, right, left, right, left, right, scrape, scrape! This may sound very funny and you may cause a laugh in the yard the first time you do it (especially if you try to knock the dust out of the curry combs – this really isn't necessary because it will fall out as you move around), but you can cut your body-brush time down by at least half.

Leather-backed brushes mould to fit your hand in time and are easier to hold, and therefore more effective in use, than wooden-backed or synthetic ones. They last, too. About six strokes on one place should be quite enough unless the horse is really dirty. You can also use the two-handed technique with dandy brushes to get off dried mud; plastic-toothed curry combs are good for this – better than rubber.

The quickest way to clean out your horse's feet is to walk him through water, but if there is none handy (and you should check for jammed-in stones and loose shoes, anyway) just use your hoofpick in the normal way, ideally from heel to toe so you don't push little stones under the loosest part of the shoe at the heels. Don't forget the sides and cleft of the frog, and automatically check for tenderness there or any foul smell which could indicate thrush developing.

Time and energy can also be saved by using grooming machines, and by rinsing the horse off with warm, clear water. Soap or shampoo is not necessary unless the horse is very greasy or dirty, and it can remove too much natural oil from the hair. In suitable weather, a simple hosing or sluicing down with a soft brush (a water-brush being the obvious choice), which is more efficient than a sponge, will clean the horse of sweat, mud and some grease.

The most effective type of electric groomer is the type which comprises a rotary brush *and* a vacuum facility, but the rotary-brush type on its own is next best. For very dusty horses, such as those covered with dried mud, a vacuum facility is a great advantage.

Dealing with mud can be a big problem for working horse owners. If the horse is out in wet, muddy conditions and you are pushed for time when you get to the stables, you will almost certainly not be able to get him dry and tack or harness on in time to exercise him. This alone is an excellent reason for using a New Zealand rug. A lightweight waterproof sheet shaped to fit the horse and with properly adjusted leg straps will keep him dry without too much warmth if the weather is mild or the horse unclipped, and will save you a lot of time and effort. Just make sure mud is cleaned off the girth area so you do not encourage rubbing and galls.

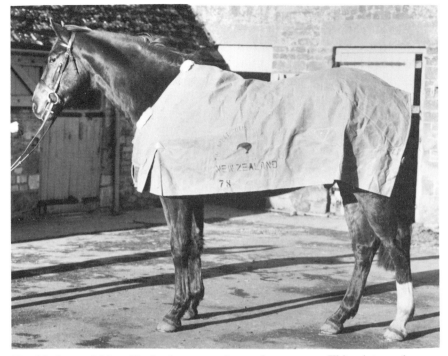

Fig. 25 A good New Zealand rug can be an investment. This picture shows a well-fitting, well-shaped rug of generous fit (well forward of the withers, not on top of them, and beyond the root of the tail) allowing plenty of roomy comfort for the horse to move about. Such a rug is an excellent way of ensuring a mud-free back when you haven't time to wait for the horse to dry. Some owners also like to use a neck hood to protect mane and neck. This rug is 'The Real McCoy' marketed by The Lavenham Rug Co. Ltd of Long Melford, Suffolk.

A neck hood may be a helpful addition to a horse's turn-out wardrobe as this will certainly keep mud off the neck and mane and so save a lot of cleaning-up time. There are head-and-neck hoods as well although I find that some horses do not like their heads being covered and the head is much less trouble to clean than the neck and mane. The neck hood is usually co-ordinated with the turn-out rug as it needs to fasten to it and overlap the neckline so that water will not seep underneath but with some types of closely-fitting hoods this may not be necessary.

I have many a time put tack on a wet (not muddy) back and gone out. I have never been able to see the difference between a back wet with sweat under the saddle and one wet with rain. An absorbent numnah between horse and saddle (cotton fleece, quilted cotton or real sheepskin) makes the horse more comfortable and absorbs moisture. Numnahs and saddle cloths are available in synthetic textiles which are said to 'wick' (draw) moisture away from the horse through the fabric, so keeping the horse drier. Regular use of a numnah anyway means you will not need to clean your saddle quite so often. When faced with a muddy back, I have also hosed off the mud, gone to work with the sweat scraper, old towels and maybe the hairdryer until the worst of the wet is gone, then saddled up, with numnah, and taken the horse out – and I have never had any problems at all or seen any sign that the horse has been uncomfortable. You can use an absorbent (lampwick) girth, too. Again, 'wicking' synthetic textiles are used for girths to help keep the horse drier under them. The girth region in particular is susceptible to softening of the skin (which then becomes more prone to rubbing and galling) so anything which helps reduce this problem is worthwhile.

Still on the topic of mud, I once received a telling-off from a vet because, having presented him with a case of mud fever, I told him all the horse books said to let mud dry under bandages, then brush it off. He told me we horse owners were all lazy, slovenly and misguided. 'You're just asking for trouble,' he said. 'Rinse it off! You have to get rid of it quickly if your horse is prone to mud fever. Dry the legs properly and you'll have no more trouble.' He was right; I didn't. He also recommended an emollient barrier cream as a preventative in susceptible individuals. Liquid paraffin is also useful for making sensitive skin water resistant. Prise the top off a clean washing-up liquid bottle, pour the liquid paraffin in and put the top back on, and you have a handy applicator.

It is a moot point whether or not to use water on horses in winter. Some people do it and, provided the horse is kept warm and dry afterwards, they have no problem. Others never do it but wait until the mud is dry, then brush it off – and similarly never have any problems! I belong to the former category, partly because I feel it best to get the horse clean as quickly as possible with the least amount of work. I do prefer lukewarm water, but cold is better than nothing if you are quick. Cavalry regiments and police stables follow this practice, as do hunt stables and many other categories of equestrian yards, all with no problem provided the horses *are* dried properly and kept warm afterwards. A heat lamp is a big advantage.

If you thatch a horse to get him dry and cool, you might find that he dries off quicker with an anti-sweat rug on top of the straw rather than an ordinary rug. The idea of the straw is to keep the horse warm so that the moisture will evaporate fairly quickly; the

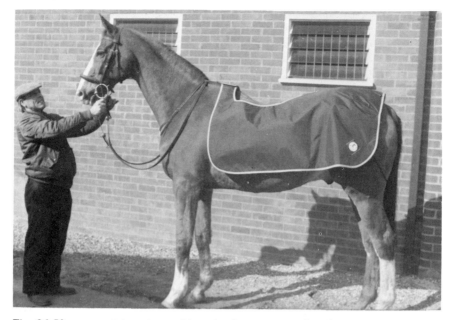

Fig. 26 If you want to return with a dry horse on a rainy day, use a waterproof exercise sheet, like this one by Lavenham. Only the shoulders get wet and they dry off naturally much quicker than the more vulnerable loins, back and quarters.

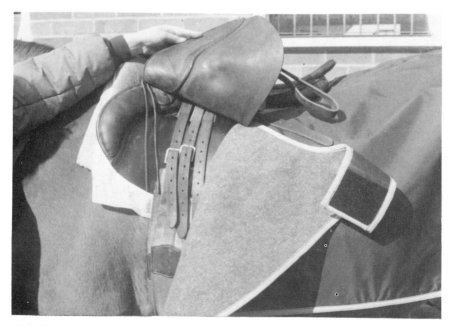

Fig. 27 Tack up in the normal way and fit the rug round the saddle and under the flap, as shown, fastening it on top of the withers.

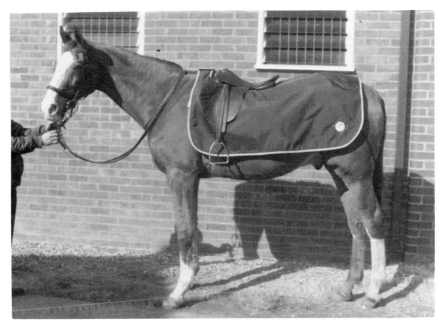

Fig. 28 The exercise sheet in place. If used at shows, for example, it can be quickly removed without having to unsaddle. The use of such a sheet means you don't have to thatch your horse and wait for him to dry off before rugging up normally.

anti-sweat rug lets it evaporate more effectively and quickly than a closer-woven rug. If you do as is often recommended and put a rug on top of the straw inside out, you may find that the moisture gathers into droplets on top of the rug (which is obviously the lining if the rug is inside out), making it damp. If you subsequently turn the rug the right way out, again as recommended, and rug the horse with it, you are rugging him up with a damp rug – hardly good stable management. Using an anti-sweat rug you do not have this problem and keep your stable/night rug dry.

If you use fabrics which are said to 'breathe' (which means that they allow moisture from the horse to evaporate up through them but prevent rain soaking through) you can, instead of conventionally thatching a horse, simply put an anti-sweat rug on and the rug on top, and the horse will dry off well. This method is especially useful in yards where straw is not used for bedding and is therefore not available for thatching. With permeable rugs the anti-sweat rug is not essential in practice but seems to help a little with some rugs.

If you do want to wash your horse in cold weather, just do a bit at a time, drying off in between, and keep the other parts of the horse covered with old rugs while you work. Hosing off a sweaty horse in summer is a refreshing way to cool him. He will cool off quicker if you use warmish water rather than cold. Horses sweat to enable them to lose body heat by the sweat evaporating into the atmosphere. If cold water is used, we cause the surface veins to constrict, holding less blood and passing less heat to the outside; so the horse will take longer to cool off. Warm water encourages the evaporation, does not shock the horse as cold water can on a hot body (particularly over muscle-mass areas like loins and quarters where the application of cold water can cause cramp) and cleans the animal better than cold.

There is no doubt that a range of good clothing can be of great help in horse management, partly in helping to keep the horse clean and dry and also to help keep him warm.

The advantages of a New Zealand rug have already been mentioned. Two should really be acquired so you can keep them both reasonably clean, the linings brushed or preferably vacuumed and the leg straps well oiled if of leather. Exercise clothing is also useful in wet weather so you do not have to wait while the horse dries off before rugging him up normally or putting his New Zealand on again to go out into the field. It is not a good plan to put a New Zealand rug on a horse with a wet coat as, with most types of New Zealand which are of the 'non-breathing' type, the water from the horse will have nowhere to evaporate to and he could stay damp under the rug for a long time and become chilled. The skin is more susceptible to rubbing when wet, too.

Synthetic fabrics save a lot of time in laundering; they dry much more quickly than natural fabrics and are lighter for the horse. At times when he is casting, a cotton or linen summer sheet next to the horse under his normal clothing helps prevent the latter becoming matted with hairs which work their way into the fabric and can be impossible to remove entirely. If woollen clothing is used, the sheet can help keep them cleaner so you are not faced with the job of washing thick, heavy clothing so often.

If your horse is clipped at all, you are almost sure to need rugs. If he is doing nothing but light work at weekends in winter, perhaps you could get away with no clip at all, or just a breast clip, where the hair is removed only from the front of the breast and up the gullet. This will be better than no clip at all if he is doing some work but, particularly with a horse of common or pony blood, could still mean you do not have problems about keeping him warm at other times.

With a trace clip, it is often overlooked that the hair has been removed from the very part of the horse which contacts the mud when he lies down: the underside. This means his skin has little protection there, so I feel it is quite wrong to think a trace-clipped horse with a New Zealand rug will be quite alright out all winter without anywhere dry such as a bedded shelter to lie down out of the weather.

It is much cheaper to keep your horse warm and in good condition by clothing him and sensibly housing and sheltering him than to do so by feeding him large amounts of concentrates. With cattle, it has been found that those kept well housed (warm but with good ventilation) ate up to 25% less concentrate than those living out, and although I have no figures for horses it seems reasonable to suppose that similar figures could apply. A shelter the horse can use if he wishes, rather than huddling behind a hedge for comfort, can make all the difference.

Horses do not feel the actual cold as much as we seem to. Studies in the U.S.A. have shown that horses can tolerate dry, still, cold weather down to −20°C (one study said −40°C) before showing signs of significant stress. However, I have often seen Thoroughbred-type horses on an autumn day, which could be described as no more than chilly but accompanied by wind and rain, who were shivering hard and could not wait to be brought in. Wind and rain exert what is called a 'chill factor' which intensifies the cold and can cause considerable suffering even in hardy breeds. Forcing horses to endure such conditions is cruel and uneconomical as it is almost impossible to feed them enough food to keep weight on; shelter is essential and good clothing highly desirable.

It is up to each owner to decide what is best for his or her own horse, but I believe it is far cheaper and more effective in the long run to buy good-quality clothing and use it when appropriate than to spend extra money on more food in cold weather. Good clothing lasts many years when properly looked after and will recoup its cost in saved feed many times over, particularly when you take into account the effects of inflation and poor harvests which push prices of feed sky high.

With any clothing, good fit is important. Stress to the supplier that you want a rug which is shaped along the spine seam to fit the

Fig. 29 Good, well-fitting clothing not only adds to your horse's comfort but saves on feed by conserving body heat provided by the food the horse eats. It would probably take only one moderately severe winter to recoup in feed costs the price of a good rug, and the rug will last many years if properly cared for. Modern synthetic rugs are easy to launder and are lighter for the horse to wear. This one, the 'Cosy Rug' by Lavenham, is shaped to fit the horse and has cross-over surcingles which increase his comfort by doing away with the conventional surcingle round the girth. Lavenham also make under blankets which fasten at the breast and stay in place without any other fastening under these rugs.

shape of the horse's back, not cut in a straight line allowing no room for the withers and croup. Rugs should come in front of the withers, not on top of them, and should extend back to the root of the tail. New Zealand rugs should go about 6 inches (15 cms) past the root of the tail, and some of the best have a drawstring sewn into the back edge of the rug which can be pulled to attain an individual fit.

When the breast straps are fastened, the neckline of the rug should rest round the base of the neck, not come down on to the shoulders. You should be able to pass your hand comfortably round the neckline and should not detect any pull on the points of the shoulders. With New Zealand or other turn-out rugs, the horse must be able to get his head down comfortably to graze without pulling the rug on to his withers or half choking himself. At the same time, the breast strap must not be so loose that it allows the rug to slip back unreasonably (although most rugs slip back a little). Modern rugs without round-the-girth surcingles but with various designs of leg straps or with diagonally-crossing under-belly surcingles are far preferable to the old-fashioned kind which act like a belt round the horse's middle and which inevitably cause some pressure on the spine.

Bedding

Apart from giving your horse somewhere comfortable to lie, good bedding in shelter or stable also helps keep him warm and so, in its own way, reduces feed costs. It also protects the horse from possible bruising on hard floors.

As mentioned, deep litter is undoubtedly the most labour and money-saving method of bedding down horses. The longest I have left a deep-litter stable (straw) was six months over winter, but I know people who have had them down for years without changing them. I have visited them regularly and have never noticed any smell, dampness, foot trouble, vermin or other disadvantages or problems. It is most noticeable that when you walk into the box or shelter it is just like stepping on to an interior-sprung mattress, springy and firm at the same time, and the horses are always quite happy on them. Sawdust, perhaps surprisingly, also makes good deep-litter bedding, but shredded paper is recommended for semi-deep litter only. Shavings scatter more easily than sawdust but are acceptable if the horse is not prone to digging up his bed.

The secret of success in deep litter is to be meticulous about removing droppings. If you miss the odd pile here and there (particularly in an open shed where you may feel it is not quite so important) you will find that your bed soon turns into an indoor muck heap – not what you want at all.

Deep litter is perhaps more suited to winter than summer in most circumstances, and ventilation is always extremely important. With long established beds, you eventually reach the stage where you are hardly adding any fresh material at all, so the bed seems to stop getting higher yet remains firm, clean and warm.

Fig. 30 A handy sized high pressure cleaner to help make light work of cleaning
down stables, yards, trailers, cars and walls. You can also meter detergents and
disinfectants into the spray for added hygiene, particularly after illness or before
and after foaling. Other models, plus various attachments, are available. Details
of this equipment are available from KEW Industry Ltd, KEW House, Gilwilly
Industrial Estate, Penrith, Cumbria, Freepost, CA11 9BR. The name of this
model is the KEW Hobby cleaner.

For those who do not like deep litter of any kind, the time-consuming chore of mucking out has to be done as quickly and thoroughly as possible. I find the quickest way is to take out all obvious droppings first, have a quick stamp or poke around for any piles that are covered up, then (if using straw) pile all the clean bedding in the cleanest corner. Then I separate all the half-clean bedding into another corner so I am left with the worst material. This is quickly shovelled outside en bloc into the largest barrow I can find (so I do not have to make any more trips to the muck heap than necessary) and the floor swept hard. When there is time, I wash the floor with hot water and washing soda (good deodorising properties and less caustic than lime). Then the semi-clean material is laid down, with some attempt to criss-cross the stalks (difficult with modern crumpled-up straw) for stability. The old clean straw is laid on top similarly and new material brought in, laid and banked up round the sides. Straw is returning to favour as a bedding material now that vacuumed straw is on the market with its dust and spores largely removed.

Whatever bedding system or material you prefer, the object should always be to keep it as clean and dry as possible. Some say that a damp bed is better for the horse's feet as the moisture helps keep the horn in good condition. It is true that brittle feet are more in need of moisture than oil, but perhaps it is overlooked that the moisture in bedding is not ordinary water but urine, which has a very bad effect on horn. Standing a horse in dirty, wet bedding is the quickest way to give him rotten horn and thrush, a fungus infection of the frog which causes pain and lameness. Therefore, I prefer to aim for dryness and let my horse's feet get their moisture from outside. The horse would not, anyway, want to lie in his own urine if he had a choice, so this is another reason to keep a dry bed.

Disposing of manure can be a problem in some areas. There is usually a market for straw and also peat (although the latter I find a very poor bedding material, being absorbent in the extreme and always damp and cold in winter and smelly in summer; it is also dusty, contrary to popular opinion). Shavings and sawdust are also not that difficult to get rid of. There is sometimes a problem with shredded paper as it does not seem to have been accepted yet as a manure. The suppliers of it often give advice as to how it can be sold and it is worth contacting the maker of your product on this point. Synthetic bedding materials make their appearance on the

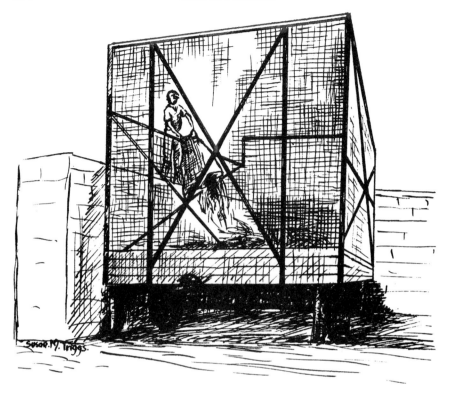

Fig. 31 An easy way to deal with muck. Try to site the muck container provided by the firm who takes away your heap in a dip so you can simply empty your barrow or muck down into it and do not have the extra work of heaving muck up from the floor or barrow to the top of the heap. This large container is in use in a commercial yard of 90 horses (a racing stable) but the idea can be adopted in any suitably structured premises.

market from time to time and can certainly be tried but it is a good plan to check with the manufacturers first exactly what is the situation regarding getting rid of the resulting manure. Being synthetic, the bedding material will presumably not rot down and will be unsuitable for manure, and it is now extremely ecologically unfriendly to burn it (and have garden or refuse bonfires at all, incidentally) and may even result in prosecution in some areas.

Mushroom and gardening nurseries often purchase bedding, and a word with other horse owners or a bit of 'finger-walking' in your Yellow Pages directory could locate a market. If you use the system of mucking out which I prefer, i.e. making two piles, one comprising almost entirely droppings and the other used bedding, you will find the droppings pile relatively easy to get rid of and the

Fig. 32 If your yard is as flat as a pancake, try this arrangement instead. Have a ramp and platform constructed next to your muck trailer so that you can simply pull (easier than pushing) the barrow up it (don't make it too steep), turn it round on the platform and tip the muck down into the trailer. Single wheeled barrows like this are more difficult to balance than the twin- or four-wheeled type, which also make handling large, time-saving loads quite easy.

other useable around your premises. Straw, shavings and sawdust can all be used to lay thickly on areas which become badly poached in winter such as gateways, the approach to shelters and around watering points. Your play area is an ideal place to spread it. The material will gradually dry out and rot away, being a natural organic product, so you will not end up with mountains of the stuff around the place. If you worm your horse properly, there will be no problem with worm eggs or larvae infecting the land.

The droppings pile can be ready bagged as described, reusing bedding and hay-age bags and avoiding the expense of buying sacks for the purpose. Once local gardeners know your muck really is 90% muck and not bedding, you could well find that you cannot provide enough of it! Commercial buyers, too, will prefer it to the normal product.

If you take a little care over the siting of your muck heap, you will find your work greatly lessened. You should try to site it downwind of the house or stables, for obvious reasons. It also helps greatly it if can be sited in a dip or even by a specially constructed and gently sloping ramp, so that the considerable job of heaving muck up on to the heap is avoided. The barrow can simply be tipped up and the muck will fall down on top of the heap.

If you have a regular arrangement with a nursery, say, to remove your heap, they may well provide a container or trailer which you simply fill and which they then remove, leaving another in its place. If you are going to use your used bedding on your own premises, it greatly facilitates transport if you dump it straight on to a trailer of your own, then one of the horses can cart it about where needed. There is no reason why Arab or Thoroughbred horses should not help in this way – it does not have to be a job for clodhoppers.

I have already said that caring for a muck heap is a job of the lowest priority in the life of a working owner. If I visit a yard where there is an immaculately combed, stamped-down steaming brick of manure in some discreet corner of the yard, I become a little concerned about the welfare of the horses themselves, because I cannot imagine any yard with today's time and labour-saving considerations having the scope to do such a job and still care properly for the horses.

It is true that compacting the muck heap does make it rot down more effectively and quickly, but most nurseries (particularly mushroom nurseries) want fresh, not rotted, manure, and even left to itself the heap *will* rot, if more slowly. It does not have to be rotted to be used as I have suggested.

Exercising and Fitness

Exercising is certainly the single most time-consuming task in the working owner's schedule, and also one of the most important if the horse is to be kept healthy, let alone fit. I have already stressed the great advantages of having turn-out facilities for augmenting normal exercise. In addition to the facilities already discussed, in small private yards horses are often allowed to wander about the place for a bit of 'light relief', if only one at a time to prevent shenanigans developing. However, for developing hard, physical fitness, there is no getting out of ridden or driven work, or, to some extent, loose schooling such as jumping, liberty work or lunging or long reining in short doses.

The worst months are obviously those with the shortest days, December and January, with November and February also being difficult for owners with other daytime commitments. The shortest day of the year is the 21 December, so after that you can console yourself that it is henceforth all downhill to spring, with milder weather and lighter nights. A nice thought during the snow and ice of January and February – and maybe of March and April, too!

If you can possibly arrange for some competent person to exercise your horse when you cannot, your life will of course be that much easier. Even being led from another horse (which again requires a competent horseperson – what an awful word!) is quite useful. If this is done, remember that the unridden horse must be on the left of the other horse and the pair must go on the left-hand side of the road in Britain. The old-fashioned method of going on the right-hand side of the road so that on-coming traffic can see you (and probably bump right into you) has long been superseded by advice from police forces nationwide, and this goes for leading in hand, too.

If the led horse wears his saddle minus stirrups, this will help keep his skin accustomed to the friction of tack. Tack sores are not uncommon in horses only ridden occasionally as the skin never has chance to harden up.

The amount of exercise a horse has should depend more on his needs than on his owner's inclinations or time availability, although it is often difficult to reconcile the two. An hour a day, however, is barely enough to keep a horse ticking over although, combined with turning out, it may be adequate. Working owners who have no access to turn-out facilities should, somehow, aim to get their horses exercised for two hours a day if at all possible. On restricted exercise, even in winter, concentrates may hardly be needed, especially for cob or pony types. Good hay or hay-age may supply all that is required.

Most general exercise is done at the walk, but some steady trotting and canter spins will have to be arranged (ground conditions permitting) if fitness is to be maintained. Some people disapprove of trotting on roads but, as described earlier in this book, used wisely it can be an advantage rather than a danger.

If you turn out a concentrate-fed horse in winter, you may well find that his time in the field maintains him half fit, particularly if he has company as horses keep each other on the move. Then much of your work can be done at this steady trot, lessening the total amount of time you need to spend on exercising.

In the black mornings of winter, it is very tempting not to tear yourself out of bed in what is still the middle of the night to give your horse his exercise, and if you are only going to work moderately at weekends it may well not be necessary, provided the horse can be turned free somewhere. But if you want a fairly fit horse, you will have to ride on certainly two and preferably three other days of the week, if only to keep his muscles used to carrying or pulling weight and his skin toughened up enough to withstand the inevitable pressures and friction of the best-fitting tack or harness.

There is no need to give a horse Sunday off if he has worked on Saturday, provided he has not become unduly tired. Three-day event horses do their hardest work on cross-country/steeplechase day but still have to show jump on the final day. If your horse works the same way in accordance with his state of fitness, you could give him Monday off, exercise Tuesday, Wednesday off, exercise Thursday, Friday off (which will give you a nice fresh horse for the weekend), and get away with exercising on only two working days of the week yet still have a reasonably fit horse.

All this assumes, of course, that you do have adequate turn-out facilities on the non-exercise days. I feel that it is a thoroughly bad practice to leave a horse stabled for even a day without significant exercise (and here I do not count a half hour lead in hand as significant exercise). Think about it from the horse's point of view. Imagine you dismount at, say, 4 p.m. on Sunday. You plan to give the horse Monday off, so no exercise on Monday morning. By 4 a.m. on Monday, he will have had twelve hours without exercise; by 4 p.m. on Monday, it will be twenty-four hours; by 4 a.m. on Tuesday morning, it will be a mind-boggling thirty-six hours cooped up in a box without exercise, and if you ride at 7 a.m. on Tuesday, the horse will have spent thirty-nine hours (a human's working week) without even enough physical activity to keep body and soul together. If you do not ride till 6 p.m. on Tuesday evening, the horse will have been subjected to enforced idleness of body and mind for a horrendous *fifty hours*!

That is more than two whole days. I think even *one* day without exercise is a terrible thing to do to an animal like a horse who

Fig. 33 Some form of light is essential when riding out in dusk or dark conditions. Stirrup lights are quite common, and now available is this cross-belt containing lights, marketed by Personalite Limited, PO Box 45, Barnet, Hertfordshire. It is called the RiderLight. In addition to a light, it is wise to wear the palest clothing you can, and to equip your horse's legs with reflective bandages.

thrives on and needs physical activity for even basic health.

Although three-day event horses, which I used in the earlier example, are (hopefully) super-fit and are often (regrettably) led around half the night to stop them stiffening up, with the average working owner's horse I feel there is no need to restrict your weekend's enjoyment and no call to restrict a horse's freedom on other days, never mind jeopardise his health.

Assuming you can get someone competent to exercise your horse, or even lead him to and from the field, the only possible problem might be insurance. Should someone have an accident while supervising your horse, there might be dreadful problems over insurance and compensation one way or another, so discuss your policy very carefully with your broker or company and be

Fig. 34 A horse and rider in dusk are much more visible when wearing reflective equipment which is picked up in car headlights. Here a hatband, tabard bearing a familiar road warning sign, wristbands and leg bandages are worn. Note also how the light parts of the horse's bridle stand out, although not reflective.
(Reproduced by kind permission of 'Your Horse' magazine.)

quite sure the policy covers all eventualities.

Most working owners have to do most of their exercising in dusk or dark conditions. Of course, it is generally advisable not to do so (certainly never in fog), but many have no choice. Floodlit manèges and indoor schools are super if you can get to such

Fig. 35 The same horse and rider from the rear showing the horse's reflective tail strip. A strong stirrup light would complete the picture, and by moving the right leg out away from the saddle when vehicles approach the rider would encourage them to give her and her horse a wider berth. (Reproduced by kind permission of 'Your Horse' magazine.)

facilities, but most people cannot. Therefore a few commonsense precautions could save lives.

First, although it is not actually unlawful for a horse and rider to go on roads with no lights, it is extremely stupid. A horse and vehicle must, by law, have lights. A stirrup light for a ridden horse is, I feel, absolutely essential, showing a strong white light to the front and a strong red one to the rear. This should be fitted to the right stirrup in countries where traffic drives on the left (and vice versa). The paler your clothing the better; it should be remembered that the most visible colour at night is reflective *white*, with orange, yellow or pink best for daytime.

Many saddlers and other bodies (such as the British Horse Society) can supply suitable reflective tabards, hat covers, arm/wrist bands and the like, and cycling shops sell useful reflective cross-belts and wrist lights for clearly-seen hand signals. Many of the more enterprising saddlers and tack stores now sell a wide range of items with lights as opposed to merely reflectors or reflective strips, from belts, sashes, and stirrup lights to a hat cover with a light on the top showing white to the front and red to the rear. Studies have shown that motorists slow down significantly, too, when they pick up moving reflective items (notably the bandages or strips on the horse's legs as he goes along) as this seems to confuse them more than relatively static reflecting equipment such as strips on an exercise sheet, provided your horse's tail is not so long as to obscure them. Lights are, however, more effective and important than reflective gear, which should be used as a back-up to them.

One thing is sure: you are not safe on the roads, no matter how dependable your horse or how impeccably you follow the Highway Code, if you cannot be seen.

Exercising can prove difficult in winter if the roads become icy and bridlepaths and other areas become too waterlogged, muddy or rutted to use. Years ago, it was fairly common for horses and ponies who had to work daily to earn their owners' livings to be shod with frost nails. These are not studs but actual horseshoe nails with little 'pimples' of hardened metal on the ground surface of the nail. Such nails are used to shoe horses who race on frozen lakes in Switzerland and Canada and similar countries, so it could be worthwhile discussing the matter with your farrier to see if they could facilitate exercising for you in icy conditions.

Another advantage of not being afraid to turn horses out on to hard-frozen fields in winter is that they do at least come in clean and dry!

If all else fails, you will have to use that pile of used bedding to lay a track round your yard or somewhere else suitable, and ride the horses round that. However, if a play area is provided or you have some kind of outdoor schooling area, you will probably find that these are the last to freeze, and your used bedding spread on top anyway will make them quite useable in hard weather.

From winter, to summer. Here the main problem with turning horses out for exercise is the flies. Some of the popular repellents work for only a short time and some appear not to work at all. One product which does work is Absorbine Super-Shield (marketed by Constant Laboratories). This is what is termed a 'residual' repellent. Agricultural suppliers have stocked them for many years due to the damage caused to cattle hides by warble flies; these repellents remain active for two or three days (not hours) but if conditions are suitable (no rain and the horse not being made to sweat much) they can work for up to ten days – although a watchful eye should be kept to see that they are still working and more applied if they are not. It is best to start using them in spring before flies arrive so that a good level of protection will have built up in the coat by summertime. If you habitually wash your horse, you will have to be sure to reapply the product after each wash.

Most repellents come in spray-on containers, and it is a common objection among owners that they cannot use them because their horses are afraid of the spray. The product can always be sprayed on to a rag, of course, and wiped on that way, but why not simply train your horse to get used to it? If you can train him to get used to traffic, jumping fences and being clipped and shod, then surely he can get used to a spray. Try stuffing cotton wool in his ears and playing the radio or even singing so he cannot hear the noise of the spray. Do not spray his head, of course, but apply the repellent with a rag on ears, forelock and face. It is often the horse's eyes which receive much of the flies' attention as they feed on the discharges. Their irritations produce more discharge which in turn attracts more flies, and so it goes on. Check first with the manufacturer of whatever product you use that it is safe for sensitive areas such as around eyes and on sheath and dock areas and, if so, be sure to apply it there where protection is really needed.

You may ultimately prefer to stable your horse during the day and turn him out at night. However, there are such things as night-flying insects, too, so a repellent is still a valuable aid to your horse's comfort and well-being and should enable you to turn him out for exercise without exposing him to the attacks of insects.

If the ground becomes baked hard in summer and your horse is not shod, you may experience problems with chipped and broken feet and, as a result, a footsore horse. So it may be necessary to have the horse shod, even if he is resting, perhaps just with race exercise shoes (not actual plates which are only aluminium). Grass tips (half shoes applied only to the toes) are rarely seen these days, most farriers and owners preferring full shoes. Exercising without shoes is quite feasible provided ground conditions are relatively soft or smooth and the hooves are regularly trimmed to maintain correct balance. Smooth, hard roads are no problem but gritted, chipped or stony surfaces should be avoided. The horse needs a good diet to produce sound horn and a good foot conformation, with no flat soles or shelly horn.

A fit, regularly worked horse involves his owner in less work than does a soft, unfit one who will have to have a strict, regularly carried-out fitness programme. Grooming is also comparatively effortless on fit horses – they seem to keep much cleaner than idle ones.

A little imagination will come up with all sorts of exercise facilities to help the working owner at any time of year and provide his or her horse with enough exercise to keep him happy, healthy and contented. Such facilities have been discussed, with the exception of one other: tethering.

Tethering a horse and leaving him is, in my opinion, a very poor way to manage him. I only recommend it in this book as being a suitable way of using some spare patch of unfenced grass about the place and letting the horse have just a bit more movement than he would have in his box. Even so, the horse should only be tethered if it is certain he will not be subject to vandalism, even from the stable dog or loose ponies, and should not be left out long in adverse weather conditions such as hot sun, fly weather, rain/sleet or wind. If it is decided to try tethering, use a neck strap rather than a headcollar. Many horses seem to prefer them, do not pull on them and they are cheaper. The tether stake should be the swivel type, and be a good metre (yard) long and very firmly driven in.

Exercise is so very important to a horse that every effort should be made to provide it by any means at our disposal.

It is hoped that the methods detailed and ideas put forward in this book will be taken in the spirit in which they were intended, i.e. to help busy horse owners look after their horses properly – and perhaps, from the horses' points of view, even better than might otherwise have been the case because of the extra freedom and liberty stressed throughout. The corners I have advised cutting will not result in any deterioration in the standard of horse care, and may well be adopted by those with more time than the average working owner in order to free time for other things.

I have sometimes advised spending money to save time, and it will be appreciated that, as discussed in the book, it is indeed sometimes necessary to spend one in order to save the other. The working horse owner's most scarce commodity is usually time, although money is a close second, and the equipment I have suggested really can help get things done so much more quickly that it is usually regarded as a sound investment.

The main thing is to get your priorities right, and place the most importance on those jobs which directly affect the horse. He will then be properly and well looked after, and you should find that you can care for him in less time than you ever thought possible – and in the long run, I hope, more cheaply – to the benefit of both of you.

Appendix 1: Recipes for success

Precisely how individual horse owners actually do get their horses cared for on a day to day, hour to hour, basis can only be decided by their own individual circumstances. The following schedules are ones which I personally have used and which worked well for me. They might act as a guide to owners trying to formulate daily programmes to ensure the adequate care of horses or ponies kept in varying conditions at different times of year.

Stabled Horse

Stabled animals are not so much at the mercy of the weather as those kept out or on the combined system (partly in and partly out). The following routine, therefore, is basically applicable at any time of year for an owner with an ordinary nine-to-five job. The references to winter tasks such as fitting reflective clothing or attending to rugs can simply be ignored in summer.

Early morning: Check horse for signs of normality or otherwise. Check droppings for consistency, odour, colour and number. Check box for signs of restlessness (e.g. churned-up bedding, scrabble marks on walls) which could indicate that the horse has perhaps been cast during the night or had an attack of colic. Check hay eaten/feed finished/water drunk. All this should take you about one minute only.

Skip out droppings, or muck out leaving floor bare, depending on bedding system used. Quarter quickly and pick out feet. Tack up/harness and put to, including light and reflective clothing if appropriate. Exercise. If raining and cold, trot home to keep horse warm.

On return, put away tack and put exercise clothing (if worn) to dry. Thatch horse in winter if wet. Give very full haynet. Bed down or add new material to deep or semi-deep litter. Give two buckets of water or check automatic waterer working and clean. Give breakfast.

Leave midday feed/hay ready for helper to give, if possible.

Finally, check breakfast eaten, top up water, skip out if necessary. Leave horse in anti-sweat rug under top rug, if still damp.

Leave for work.

Midday (*if help available*): Rug up horse normally if still thatched, or readjust rugs. Skip out droppings. Feed. Top up hay/water.

Evening: Check horse quickly, as early morning. Quarter and pick out feet. Tack up/harness and put to, including lights and reflective clothing, and exercise/lunge/lead in hand to graze, as appropriate. On return, put away tack, etc. and thatch if wet. Pick out feet/check shoes. Give water and full haynet(s). Skip out and replenish/fluff up bedding. Groom if dry. Feed.

Late evening, if at all possible: Check horse, as usual. Remove thatch and rug up normally for night, or readjust rugs. Leave full haynet(s) and two buckets of water. Skip out/fluff up bedding. Feed, if required. Groom if not done before.

Leave dry feeds ready mixed for morning, fill haynet(s). Take exercise clothing home to dry.

Grass-Kept Horse

Winter

A grass-kept horse in winter needs only a little less attention than a stabled one. If he is expected to, say, hunt or do other strenuous work on Saturdays, he will still need ridden or driven work on two or three days a week to keep him fit enough. The exercise he gives himself in the field will keep him 'ticking over' but will not maintain hard fitness. A suggested daily routine for a grass-kept horse in winter, on a day when he is being ridden/driven, is as follows.

Early morning: Check horse for well-being, especially for signs of exposure ailments such as mud fever and rain rash, runny eyes/chapped face and loss of condition, and feel right through unclipped areas of coat. Tie up in shelter or spare stable and remove New Zealand rug to do this. Pick out feet and tidy up as best you can. Tack up/harness and put to, with lights and reflective clothing if needed. A light, waterproof sheet will be needed during exercise if raining, as New Zealand rug cannot be replaced on wet horse without risking chill/skin problems and you will not have time to wait for horse to dry before going to work.

On return, feed (separately from other horses if necessary), top up hay in shelter, check water supply. Skip out shelter. Replace/change New Zealand rug, padlock field gate both ends. Put away tack/harness and put exercise sheet somewhere to dry.

Evening: Check horse as morning. Quarter, paying special attention to feet and legs and underside of horse for signs of mud fever, and check for rain rash on neck/back. If possible, bring horse into box, wash off mud, rinse and dry thoroughly and apply preventative cream before returning horse to field. (This sounds over-protective, but if horse is of type susceptible to mud fever this is much less trouble, in the long run, than having to deal with actual ailment, which can be very stubborn, necessitating stabling and veterinary treatment.)

Horse can be eating feed while you do above. Also, quarter him, check feet/shoes, put on New Zealand rug and return to field. Top up hay, check water, skip out shelter and replenish bedding. Padlock gate both ends.

You will need some kind of light. Motorists' lanterns, which can be hung up somewhere while you work, are more convenient than torches.

If the horse is a very hardy type, wintering out without a New Zealand rug and maybe without a shelter either, extra vigilance will be needed on the part of the owner. The horse cannot be clipped if living in such conditions and will seldom be dry enough to get on tack or harness, so weekday exercise will be skipped. A very watchful eye must be kept for ailments and loss of condition, and the horse should be regularly quartered and feet and shoes checked/picked out daily.

Summer

Early morning: Check horse, quarter/pick out feet. Tack up/harness and put to. Exercise. On return, feed if appropriate, skip out shelter, check water supply, hay up shelter if paddock bare. Padlock gate both ends. Put away tack/harness, etc. and leave for work.

Evening: Check horse, quarter/pick out feet. If working, tack up/harness and put to and exercise. On return, feed if appropriate, skip out shelter, check water, hay up shelter if necessary. Padlock gate both ends. Put away tack/harness, etc. and leave.

Combined-System Horse

This is an ideal system for the working horse owner, winter or summer, and is certainly the one to aim at if at all possible.

Winter

The following routine is suggested for a horse who is trace or chaser clipped and whose owner works all day.

Early morning: Check horse, etc. exactly as for stabled horse. Quarter/pick out feet. If exercising, tack up/harness and put to, using lights/reflective clothing if appropriate. Exercise, using waterproof exercise sheet if raining. On return, put away tack/harness and feed horse. Put exercise clothing to dry. Put New Zealand rug on horse. Put full hay supply in shelter, check water supply and leave midday feed for helper to give, if possible. Turn horse out. Muck out, leaving floor bare, or skip out if deep litter. Leave for work.

Evening: Bed down/replenish bedding, hang up full haynet(s) and give two buckets of water or check waterer. Bring horse in, remove New Zealand rug and check horse carefully for injuries sustained in field. Quarter/groom. Rug up. Wash/cream legs as for grass-kept horse if susceptible to mud fever. Otherwise, rinse off mud, dry thoroughly and bandage legs. Take New Zealand rug home to dry.

Late evening, if possible: Check horse. Adjust rugs. Top up hay/water. Skip out/fluff up bedding. Feed, if required. Leave dry feed ready for morning.

Summer

Early morning: Bed down box/replenish bedding. Bring horse in and check. Quarter/groom/pick out feet and check shoes. If exercising, tack up/harness and put to. Exercise. On return, put away tack/harness. Give full haynet(s), water and feed. Leave horse in for day, away from flies.

Midday, if help available: Check horse, skip out box, feed/hay/water.

Evening: Check horse, feed if appropriate and turn out for night. Muck out box and leave floor bare overnight, or skip out if on deep litter (not normally recommended for summer unless box very well ventilated). Skip out shelter, replenish bedding. Check water supply. Hay up shelter if paddock bare. Padlock gate both ends.

It is stressed that these routines are only suggestions of successful ways of getting done everything which needs to be done on a daily basis. Tack/harness cleaning can be done as and when there is time – at home in the evening rather than wasting 'stables' time. Other jobs can be fitted in, probably at weekends, or on days when no exercising is taking place in the case of the grass-kept or combined-system horse. Many owners may prefer to exercise horses in the latter category (who normally only need exercising once a day) in the evening rather than the morning, but the routines are flexible enough to be altered to suit individual requirements. The important point is that all essential jobs are listed and, by following these routines and fitting them in with your own daily timetable, you can be sure you are doing everything necessary to care for your horse adequately.

Appendix 2: Do you *really* need to call the vet?

Veterinary surgeons cost money but their services are essential not only in curing sickness and in treating injuries but in helping, by means of preventive medicine, to keep our horses healthy. Most horse owners are, at some time or other, presented with a situation where they do not know whether they really need to call the vet or not. If they delay the horse could become worse and treatment more prolonged and expensive, or the delay could even kill the horse. If they call the vet and the situation turns out to be something or nothing, or rights itself just as the vet arrives (!) they have wasted a not inconsiderable visit fee and the vet's time which could have been more usefully spent on some more urgent matter.

The following flow charts are designed to help you decide whether or not to bring in the vet now or wait and see how things develop. *It cannot be overstressed, however, that if you are in doubt you are far better to call the vet, or at least telephone him or her for advice, than to risk aggravating a potentially serious condition through delay.*

Some symptoms apply to many different disorders and whilst diagnosis is the vet's job, owners or those attending animals regularly are in the best position to know, or simply sense, that an animal is not quite 'right' and should be watched at least. These charts cannot cover every eventuality but they cover the main signs which should alert your attention and it is hoped they will provide a quick and easy aid to making the right decision.

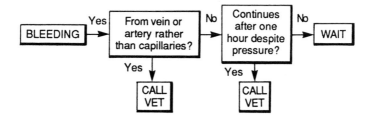

Flow chart 1   Bleeding

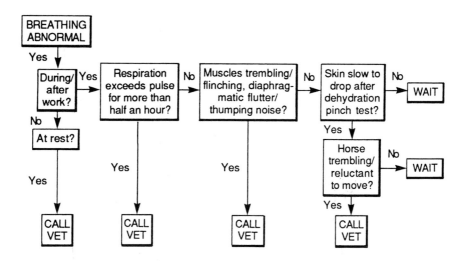

Flow chart 2   Respiration

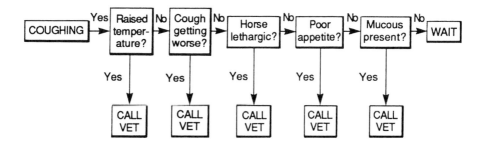

Flow chart 3   Coughing

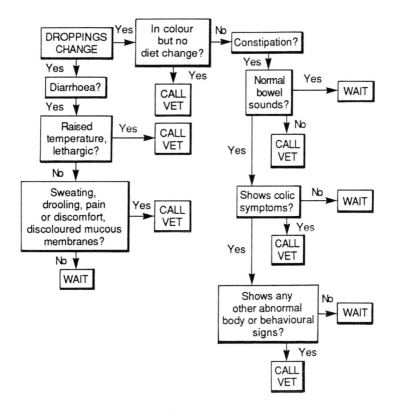

Flow chart 4   Digestive and gastric abnormalities

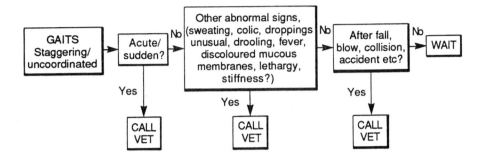

Flow chart 5   Abnormal gait

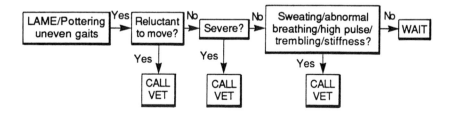

Flow chart 6   Lameness

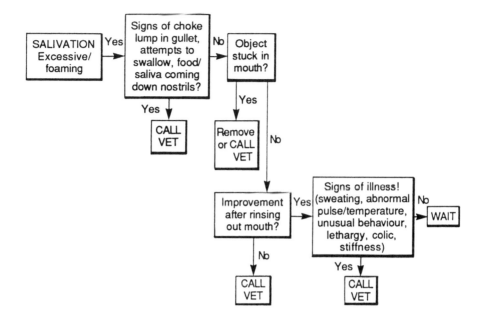

Flow chart 7   Salivation or choking

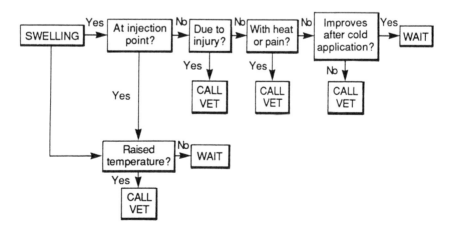

Flow chart 8   Swelling

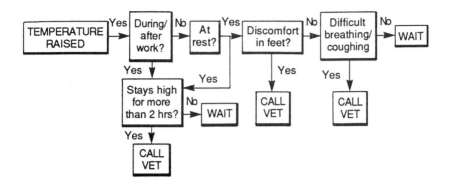

Flow chart 9   Abnormal temperature

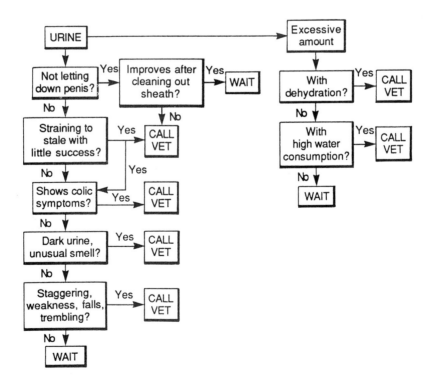

Flow chart 10   Urinary symptoms

Index

BLACKWELL SCIENTIFIC PUBLICATIONS

List of available books

Horse and Stable Management
Jeremy Houghton-Brown and Vincent Powell-Smith
"A new classic ... a clearly written and easily understood handbook" *Riding*
"We greatly welcome its publication ... sure to become a standard work of reference for horse owners and students and we give it our unreserved recommendation." *Stable Management*
256 pages, illustrated paperback.
0 632 02141 1

Getting Horses Fit
Second Edition
Sarah Pilliner
This book is aimed at trainers, riders and owners who want to increase their knowledge of the horse's body systems during exercises and devise suitable training programmes for disciplines as diverse as long distance riding and 3 day eventing. "A really outstanding book ... it is sure to become one of the most important and sought-after books on horses published in recent years as an authoritative and reliable guide." *Stable Management*
256 pages, illustrated paperback.
0 632 034769

The Equine Athlete
How to develop your horse's athletic potential
Jo Hodges and Sarah Pilliner
A comprehensive and practical guide to developing the athletic performance of competition horses.
222 pages, illustrated hardback.
0 632 02622 7

The Competition Horse
Susan McBane and Gillian McCarthy
Surveys the whole field of producing, breeding, managing and developing competition horses for major sports.
261 pages, illustrated hardback.
0 632 02327 9

Pasture Management for Horses and Ponies
Gillian McCarthy
"For anyone interested in keeping their grazing in good condition." *Horse and Rider*. A practical handbook providing guidance on how to manage the land available to best advantage.
272 pages, illustrated paperback.
0 632 02286 8

Equine Injury, Therapy and Rehabilitation
Second Edition
Mary Bromiley
"I would recommend to anyone her refreshingly modern and practical approach to the healing of horse injuries" *Captain Mark Phillips*
"An excellent book for all horse owners" *Horse and Rider*
"Essential reading for all owners and trainers as well as veterinary surgeons and physiotherapists" *Hoofprint*
The author explains basic anatomy linked to common sites of injury, the modern approach to healing horse injuries, how to spot injuries and observe the responses to vet's treatment and machines available to rehabilitate horses.
160 pages, illustrated paperback.
0 632 03608 7

Horse Business Management
Jeremy Houghton-Brown and Vincent Powell-Smith
At any level of horse ownership there is always a need for business expertise and skill to manage your equine investment. The book is full of practical ideas which have been proved to achieve good results.
208 pages, illustrated hardback.
0 632 02184 5

Breeding the Competition Horse
Second Edition
John Rose and Sarah Pilliner
This practical guide covers all aspects of breeding and stud management, incorporating the most up-to-date scientific principles. It will prove invaluable both for the busy professional stud owner as well as the owner of a single mare.
220 pages, illustrated hardback.
0 632 03727 X

How to Keep your Horse Healthy
Colin Vogel
Essential reading for all who care for horses professionally and generally as well as students.
156 pages, illustrated paperback.
0 632 02056 3